Ontological Branding

Philosophy of Race

Series Editor: George Yancy, Emory University

Editorial Board: Sybol Anderson, Barbara Applebaum, Alison Bailey, Chike Jeffers, Janine Jones, David Kim, Emily S. Lee, Zeus Leonardo, Falguni A. Sheth, Grant Silva

The Philosophy of Race book series publishes interdisciplinary projects that center upon the concept of race, a concept that continues to have very profound contemporary implications. Philosophers and other scholars, more generally, are strongly encouraged to submit book projects that seriously address race and the process of racialization as a deeply embodied, existential, political, social, and historical phenomenon. The series is open to examine monographs, edited collections, and revised dissertations that critically engage the concept of race from multiple perspectives: sociopolitical, feminist, existential, phenomenological, theological, and historical.

Recent Titles in the Series

Ontological Branding: Power, Privilege, and White Supremacy in a Colorblind World, by Bonard Iván Molina García

Black Men from Behind the Veil: Ontological Interrogations, by George Yancy

White Educators Negotiating Complicity: Roadblocks Paved with Good Intentions, by Barbara Applebaum

White Ignorance and Complicit Responsibility: Transforming Collective Harm Beyond the Punishment Paradigm, by Eva Boodman

Iranian Identity, American Experience: Philosophical Reflections on Race, Rights, Capabilities, and Oppression, by Roksana Alavi

The Weight of Whiteness: A Feminist Engagement with Privilege, Race, and Ignorance, by Alison Bailey

The Logic of Racial Practice: Explorations in the Habituation of Racism, edited by Brock Bahler

Hip-Hop as Philosophical Text and Testimony: Can I Get a Witness?, by Lissa Skitolsky

The Blackness of Black: Key Concepts in Critical Discourse, by William David Hart

Self-Definition: A Philosophical Inquiry from the Global South and Global North, by Teodros Kiros

A Phenomenological Hermeneutic of Antiblack Racism in The Autobiography of Malcolm X, by David Polizzi

Buddhism and Whiteness, edited by George Yancy and Emily McRae

Black Christology and the Quest for Authenticity: A Philosophical Appraisal, by John H. McClendon III

Ontological Branding

Power, Privilege, and White Supremacy in a Colorblind World

Bonard Iván Molina García

LEXINGTON BOOKS
Lanham • Boulder • New York • London

Published by Lexington Books
An imprint of The Rowman & Littlefield Publishing Group, Inc.
4501 Forbes Boulevard, Suite 200, Lanham, Maryland 20706
www.rowman.com

86-90 Paul Street, London EC2A 4NE

Copyright © 2022 by The Rowman & Littlefield Publishing Group, Inc.

Parts of Chapter 3 are reproduced from BLACK BODIES, WHITE GAZES: THE CONTINUING SIGNIFICANCE OF RACE IN AMERICA, Second Edition by George Yancy - Foreword by Linda Martin Alcoff, published by Rowman & Littlefield Publishers. © The Rowman & Littlefield Publishing Group, Inc., 2016. Reproduced by arrangement with The Rowman & Littlefield Publishing Group

All rights reserved. No part of this book may be reproduced in any form or by any electronic or mechanical means, including information storage and retrieval systems, without written permission from the publisher, except by a reviewer who may quote passages in a review.

British Library Cataloguing in Publication Information Available

Library of Congress Cataloging-in-Publication Data

Names: Molina García, Bonard Iván, author.
Title: Ontological branding : power, privilege, and white supremacy in a colorblind world / Bonard Iván Molina García.
Description: Lanham : Lexington Books, [2022] | Series: Philosophy of race | Includes bibliographical references.
Identifiers: LCCN 2022026698 (print) | LCCN 2022026699 (ebook) | ISBN 9781666902358 (cloth) | ISBN 9781666902372 (paperback) | ISBN 9781666902365 (ebook)
Subjects: LCSH: Race awareness—United States. | White people—Race identity—United States. | Racial justice—United States. | Racism—United States. | Race—Philosophy. | Ontology. | Phenomenology. | United States—Race relations.
Classification: LCC E184.A1 M625 2022 (print) | LCC E184.A1 (ebook) | DDC 305.800973—dc23/eng/20220727
LC record available at https://lccn.loc.gov/2022026698
LC ebook record available at https://lccn.loc.gov/2022026699

*To Jeanné, Lydia, and the St. Augustine
Social Justice Book Club.*

Contents

Introduction		1
1	Tool Ontology	7
2	Ontological Brands	21
3	A Genealogy of (White) America	33
4	The Pale and Inconspicuous Presence	83
5	Ontological Justice as Racial Justice	111
Conclusion		127
Bibliography		131
Index		137
About the Author		141

Introduction

This project began with my wife, Gaela, and I reading Michelle Alexander's *The New Jim Crow* with the book club at St. Augustine Church in Washington D.C. Gaela and I, both attorneys, were gutted to see, page after page, blatant and rampant legal injustices about which we knew nothing. Nobody taught us in law school. In our decades of legal practice, it just had not come up. As we read and discussed, a single question emerged for me, over and over, the same one, a common thread that ran through the world we explored in the book club as well as through the world of my own experience: what is race?

Gaela and I attended St. Augustine because it felt like home. St. Augustine is a historically Black Catholic church. Gaela and I are Latinx. Nonetheless, despite having come to the United States as an undocumented Mexican immigrant, most Americans think I am white when they first meet me. To most American eyes, as I have been told many times, *I just don't look Mexican*. Growing up in the United States, I, like so many other kids, went to public schools that were racially diverse in terms of absolute numbers but far less diverse within the tracks for so-called gifted and talented kids. It was not unusual for me to be the only Latinx student in my class. Sometimes I was the only person of color. *Person of color*. But how could that be since, as I have also been told, I have no color? Fast forward to the St. Augustine book club. Gaela and I are in the sacred space of exploring difficult truths with our church family, and I get a glimpse, for the first time, of Black being in the world, specifically, of Black being in the world that is (white) America. So there I am, a Mexican immigrant, often treated like he's white, in a Black world that is family and feels like home, within a white world that has become home and often treats me like I belong while treating my family like it does not.

What is race? Heidegger noted that asking what something is is inseparable from asking what it is for. We are constantly moving through our worlds, learning and using the tools we need to go about building and living our lives. And so, as I embarked on my exploration of what race *is*, what began to be revealed was what race is *for*. In this book, I argue that race is a tool. Specifically, race is a way of ontologically branding certain persons as subordinate for the sake of privileging the unbranded with personhood in a world where all (and only) persons get to be equal.[1] In the contemporary United States, race works to privilege whiteness by branding persons of color, particularly Black persons, as subordinate and properly restricted to ways of being in service to the (white) world. In America, white persons are the protagonists in the story of an egalitarian liberal democracy that has steadily marched in the direction of greater and greater freedom, equality, and justice. Meanwhile, persons of color, especially Black persons, are supposed to fade into the invisible background of that story. If persons of color know their place and stay in it, they may be permitted to live out their lives, perhaps even rewarded. But if they do not, they cease to be invisible; they become obtrusive and court the gaze of a (white) America in which persons of color, especially Black persons, are subject to a constant threat of violence and death.

This white supremacist world, what I term (white) America, was created and has been protected by U.S. law.[2] Current U.S. law, of course, would deny such a charge and point out that, in fact, the exact opposite is true. U.S. law, after all, has rejected the white supremacist social ontology it once espoused, and it is precisely because the law now appreciates that race does *not* matter and that we now live in an era where racial justice is understood to be the disregarding of race. As Supreme Court Chief Justice John Roberts succinctly put it, "[t]he way to stop discrimination on the basis of race is to stop discriminating on the basis of race."[3] This approach is predicated on an ontological lie: that in the United States, all persons are equal. If all persons are equal, after all, race does not matter, and justice means treating everyone the same way, regardless of race. But in the United States, all persons are not equal. In the United States, only some enjoy the privilege of being a person simpliciter. Most are ontologically demoted and have restricted access to the benefits of being a person as such. One of the ways persons are ontologically demoted is through race. Race in the United States operates as a tool to brand certain persons as ontologically subordinate for the sake of privileging the unbranded with full personhood in a world by and for persons. Whiteness is the state of being unbranded, and white privilege is the privilege of getting to be a person in a world where persons of color are excluded from full membership in personhood. White privilege is about getting to be white in a white supremacist world.

The ontological hierarchy that governs whiteness and nonwhiteness is the foundation of American white supremacy. This hierarchy was created by and is preserved through U.S. law. In antebellum America, U.S. law expressly espoused a white supremacist social ontology according to which nonwhite persons were properly excluded from the "We" of the "We the People." During that time, the United States exploded in economic and global stature while persons of color, especially Black persons, were devalued, exploited, and subject to a constant threat of violence and death. In the Jim Crow era, even after the Reconstruction Amendments, U.S. law continued its espousal of an expressly white supremacist social ontology according to which law had no business intervening in social inequalities that existed because the races were unequal by nature. During that time, the United States continued its rise in economic and global stature while persons of color, especially Black persons, continued to be devalued, exploited, and subject to a constant threat of violence and death.

U.S. law underwent major changes through Reconstruction and the Civil Rights era, but the technology of racial subordination evolved in tandem so that law has consistently protected and advanced the interests of white supremacy. In the current era of colorblindness, U.S. law continues to safeguard white supremacy even as it proclaims to have replaced a white supremacist social ontology with one in which race is meaningless because all persons are equal. As current U.S. law tells it, problems arise out of deliberate racial discrimination through specific governmental acts, and the solution is thus the erasure of race from governmental decision-making. But white supremacy does not depend on deliberate discrimination or specific governmental acts. In fact, white supremacy constitutes such a normal part of ordinary, everyday life in the United States that it is largely invisible, especially to those privileged by it. In other words, white supremacy is largely invisible to the very persons who hold the reins of power over a legal system that preserves white supremacy and safeguards their hold on those very reins.

U.S. law's current approach to racial justice depends on ontological legerdemain. By acting as if race is meaningless because all persons are equal, U.S. law attempts to define away the entrenched racial disparities it has created and maintained over the past 400 years. By defining persons as equal per se vis-à-vis race, U.S. law is free to look at rampant racial inequalities and blame them on persons of color themselves. After all, since all are equal, since the law sees only individuals and their private choices, and since law is bound to respect these choices, any appearance of racial inequality is an illusion because there are no racial groups to speak of. There are only individuals, and if certain individuals make choices that result in poverty, criminality, lack of education, or poor health, these individuals have only themselves to blame. The law is powerless to intervene in the realm of private choices. The result is a (white) America that sees itself as largely egalitarian even as the empirical data flooding us over the past decades confirms what persons of color have been repeating for centuries: persons of color, especially Black persons, continue to be devalued, exploited, and subject to a constant threat of violence and death.

In the United States today, nonwhite lives, and especially Black lives, matter less. This is the result of a legal system that created and protected white supremacy by codifying an understanding that—as Jefferson Davis once argued—the "inequality of the white and black races" has been "stamped from the beginning."[4] Racial justice, thus, cannot be served by U.S. law now deciding to turn a blind eye to race. Instead, as Justice Sonia Sotomayor corrected, what is needed "is to speak openly and candidly on the subject of race, and to apply the Constitution with eyes open to the unfortunate effects of centuries of racial discrimination."[5] Racial justice requires a critical race consciousness that accounts for the ontology of race. Racial justice requires ontological justice. Until U.S. law acknowledges that all persons are not equal because white persons enjoy a privileged status while nonwhite persons are subordinated within a white supremacist system the law itself has created and maintained, none of the developments in legal equality will meaningfully strike at the roots of racial injustice. As Kate Manne has argued, if we want to change the world, we may need to conceptualize it differently.[6]

In chapter 1, I provide an overview of Heidegger's tool ontology. In chapter 2, I introduce the ontological brand, my term for a tool used to designate certain persons as subordinate persons for the sake of privileging the unbranded with personhood simpliciter. I argue that in the United States race is an ontological brand that designates persons of color—particularly Black persons—as subordinate persons. By doing so, the unbranded, that is, white persons, are privileged with personhood simpliciter in a world where all (and only) persons are equal. Because race is such a familiar part of everyday American life, the subordinating and privileging functions of race operate in a largely invisible way to most of us. Race is an exercise of ontological power, that is, determining who gets to count as a person and who does not. Ontological branding is not restricted to race, however, and I discuss the application of the ontological branding model to other intersecting systems of subordination based on visible identities.

In chapter 3, I provide a brief genealogy of white supremacy in America. I argue that race emerged as an ontological brand in the West to resolve the tension created by the simultaneous development of the Enlightenment, with its ideals of universal human equality and colonialism, which entailed horrendous abuses, enslavement, and genocide. The invention of race resolved this tension by ontologically branding non-Europeans as subordinate entities. In the United States, persons of African descent were all branded with the same brand of blackness that designated them as the quintessential subordinate beings. Black persons were thus excluded from full participation in personhood and were instead reduced to roles in service to (white) America. The boundary between whiteness and blackness began with U.S. law creating a white right to harm Black persons. This right to harm existed to exploit Black persons and punish them for stepping outside of their permitted spaces. This right to harm is the foundation of white privilege, a privilege that U.S. law continues to protect despite a formally colorblind legal system.

In chapter 4, I explore the phenomenology of Black subordination and white privilege in contemporary (white) America. Persons of color are ontologically subordinated such that their ways of being (allowed to be) in the world are restricted to roles in service to (white) America. Meanwhile, white persons enjoy the ontological privilege of having nearly unlimited access to ways of being in a world made by and for them. Persons of color thus face an ever-present impossible choice between accepting their ontological constraints or challenging them in a white supremacist world that subjects them to the constant threat of violence and death.

In chapter 5, I argue that racial justice requires ontological justice, that is, a critical, race-conscious, affirmative dismantling of the ontological privilege of whiteness. Because the white supremacy that permeates (white) America is created and maintained through U.S. law, I suggest ways in which law itself can help move us from a (white) America to the America we claim to be, an America for us all.

NOTES

1. I largely avoid the term "racism" because, as Charles Mills puts it, "the term is now used in such a confusingly diverse range of ways that it is difficult to find a stable semantic core." Charles Mills, *Black Rights/White Wrongs: The Critique of Racial Liberalism* (New York: Oxford University Press, 2017), 117. I focus instead on "racial injustice, the distinctive injustice of the modern world." Mills, *Black Rights/White Wrongs*, 139. Much has been written on whether racial injustice concerns dehumanizing the other, where dehumanization means demoting someone in such a way that they are no longer a human being. E.g., David Livingstone Smith, *Less than human: Why We Demean, Enslave, and Exterminate Others* (New York: St. Martin's Press, 2011). As regards white supremacy, this would mean downgrading nonwhite persons to something less than human. E.g., Charles Mills, *The Racial Contract* (Ithaca: Cornell University Press, 1997). As Kate Manne notes, however, racial and gender-based subordination in the contemporary West operate not by excluding persons of color and women from humanity but by constraining them to certain permissible "all too human" ways of being and punishing them for challenging

those constraints. Kate Manne, *Down Girl: The Logic of Misogyny* (Oxford: Oxford University Press, 2018), 168; Kate Manne, "Humanism," 42 *Soc. Theory Pract.* 2 (2016): 389–415. I follow Manne's approach to frame racial injustice in terms of those who get to be a person simpliciter and those who are relegated to the status of subordinate person in service to persons as such.

2. By "law" in this book I refer to any exercise of State power deemed legitimate by the State's own standards. Law can thus include legislation, judicial decisions, or acts by agencies so long as these are recognized as legitimate by the State itself.

3. *Parents Involved in Community Schools v. Seattle School District No. 1*, 551 US 701 (2007).

4. Ibram X. Kendi, *Stamped from the Beginning: The Definitive History of Racist Ideas in America* (New York: Nation Books, 2016), 3.

5. *Schuette v. Coalition to Defend Affirmative Action*, 572 US 291, 381 (2014) (Sotomayor, J., dissenting).

6. Manne, *Down Girl*, 42.

Chapter 1

Tool Ontology

I argue that in the contemporary United States, race is best understood as a brand, much like a brand used on cattle or criminals, where the brand of race is used to designate certain persons as ontologically demoted for the sake of privileging the unbranded with full personhood in a world where all persons (and only persons) get to be equal. Under this model, whiteness is the absence of such a brand, and white privilege is getting to be a person simpliciter in a world where persons of color are excluded from full membership in personhood. Because white privilege was created by and continues to be safeguarded through law, the United States is a white supremacist system. Racial justice thus requires, in part, a reworking of U.S. law to dismantle white privilege.

To develop my argument, I apply Heideggerian tool ontology to the phenomenology of race. But why Heidegger? It seems a little awkward to turn to a Nazi for advice on dismantling white supremacy. Heidegger, however, is essential to this project both because of his particular work on tool ontology and because of his importance in the contemporary West's understanding of itself. Heidegger's work on tool ontology is unique in its exploration of the most fundamental ways in which we go about building and inhabiting worlds. This work is necessary to properly examine the various dimensions of embodied human experience that unfold within a world that is always already oriented around whiteness. But Heidegger's value is not just in providing access to the proverbial master's tools which we can use to dismantle the master's own house; Heidegger also provides valuable insight into what the master's house actually is, how it is actually built, and what it is actually founded on, despite how drastically the façade may have changed over time.

In his celebrated *Question Concerning Technology*, Heidegger warns that humanity is at risk of losing itself in a view that strips the world and its things of intrinsic value, reducing all to things valuable only inasmuch as they are useful for something.[1] Heidegger diagnoses and prophesies that humanity is at risk of becoming one more natural resource to be plundered and exploited. If, as Heidegger argues, we are what we do, what would it do to our being to have the freedom to do only what we are permitted to do in the interstices of our exploitation? At its most basic level, freedom in the modern West means the freedom to be who we are, and anything that constrains our ability to do so by reducing us to things valuable instrumentally instead of beings valuable intrinsically should receive our most urgent attention.

But Heidegger's predictions have already come to pass. It is already the case that humanity has been stripped of its intrinsic value and left only with its value as instrumental to others' ends. Humanity has already been rendered one more resource to be plundered—but it has not happened to all of humanity; this has befallen only the non-European majority of humanity, rendered part of a larger world that exists to be subdued and exploited by Europe and its heirs. Since the Enlightenment, the West has been on a proud march toward increasing human equality, and in the United States, our laws have been on a proud march toward increasingly treating all persons like they are equal. As it turns out, however, this is all within a context where "person" is a term of art that excludes most of humanity. As it turns out, the rights and privileges of being a person are available only to those who get to count as persons, and those who do not get to count as persons are valuable only inasmuch as they serve the interests of those enjoying full personhood.

The evolving façade of equality that adorns the master's house, then, has from the beginning hidden the underlying structures that support it, namely, the rendering of most of humanity as mere resources to be exploited for the sake of privileging those who count as persons with personhood as such. The freedom enjoyed by the heirs to the West is predicated on the subordination of everybody else. For the past two decades, the problem of whiteness has increasingly come to the foreground for those of us who care about race. It has been a notoriously difficult phenomenon to address because it is simultaneously everything and nothing, empty and full, one and many. Heidegger's ontology is uniquely helpful in this regard. His work on the visibility and invisibility of the most fundamental components of our experience provides valuable material with which we can model the subtle and hegemonic workings of whiteness and white supremacy.

MERE THINGS, PERSONS, AND TOOLS

In *Being and Time*, Heidegger suggests three modes of being: the being of mere things, the being of persons, and the being of tools.[2] The idea is not that these are exclusive categories; rather, these terms refer to distinct dimensions of being that overlap and interact depending on the entity examined and how that entity is approached.

We could, for example, approach the entire universe as a collection of mere things devoid of human context.[3] Colloquially, we might call this a scientific view. To approach a helium atom in this way is to see it in terms of its facts (e.g., that it contains two protons). These facts about mere things are independent of human context such that whether we study a helium atom in the United States or China, or yesterday or today, a helium atom will always have two protons. This view allows us to see, as Hubert Dreyfus explains, the "context-free features or properties" of things by "leaving out all relevance to human purposes."[4] I will refer to such a fact-centered view as an ontic view.[5] We can, of course, also adopt such a view toward persons and form an understanding of ourselves as mere things.[6] Among the mere facts about me, for example, we could include that my red blood cells lack A or B antigens. As a practical matter, facts matter to us because they help us understand the kind of thing something is (I am blood type O, helium is a noble gas), and they can tell us useful information about that thing (I should be donating blood on a regular basis, blimps should be filled with helium instead of hydrogen).

But persons are irreducible to an ontic picture, no matter how many facts we might learn about them.[7] What ultimately makes me me is not what I am but *who* I am, and this is disclosed not by the summation of mere facts about me but by what I do, how I live, and my distinct ways of being. This recognition gives rise to Heidegger's famous phrase that a person's essence is existence.[8] Under this framework, while all beings are, only persons exist. That is to say, electrons and stars are there and will be there with or without persons around to see them, but Heidegger reserves the term "existence" for persons. Existing is what we do, and this everyday, familiar activity of existing is what Heidegger calls "being-in-the-world."[9] In Heidegger's words, a person "is not distinguished by its what, like a chair in contrast to a house. Rather, this designation in its own way expresses the way to be."[10] Persons are not just a type of being but a way of being. This way of being distinguishes the ontic from the ontological.

In contrast to the ontic, the ontological dimension of being considers the significance of human context. Whereas under an ontic view, I can be regarded as an entity with particular properties, under an ontological view, I am not just a *homo sapiens* (a what) but *myself* (a who) as disclosed in my distinct way of being that self. To truly understand who I am, we first must understand my ways of being in the world. Beyond facts like my blood type, age, or place of birth, we would need to understand, for example, the ontological reality that I am a father since fatherhood informs my way of being in the world.[11]

Mere things are understood in terms of their facts. Persons are understood through our ways of being in the world. And the third mode of being Heidegger suggests, the being of tools, is defined by the role tools play in the human context.[12] The term "tool" is used here in the broadest sense, referring to anything we use in any way as we go about our lives. As Heidegger puts it, "[t]he tool has the character of being of '*in-order-to*.'"[13] A hammer is a tool, for example, and if I am a carpenter, I might use a hammer in order to drive a nail into a piece of wood.

Note how a hammer is not a mere thing. We could certainly approach the hammer in an ontic way, accumulating facts about it (e.g., dimension, weight, material properties), but just as persons are irreducible to their ontic pictures, so too are tools. Persons are understood by our distinct ways of being in the world, and tools are understood by their role in those human ways of being. As Sara Ahmed succinctly puts it, "[f]or Heidegger what makes 'the table' what it is, and not something else, is what the table allows us to do."[14] What makes a hammer a hammer, then, is that it is an in-order-to-strike, and it is that only in relation to a context of human activity. In Heidegger's words, a tool—or, as Macquarrie and Robinson translate the term, "equipment"— "always is in terms of its belonging to other equipment."[15] "Taken strictly, there 'is' no such thing as *an* equipment. To the being of any equipment there always belongs an equipmental whole, in which it can be this equipment that it is."[16] The use of tools thus implies work, which is to say, a purpose. Continuing with carpentry as an example, Heidegger explains that "[w]ith hammering there is an involvement in making something fast; with making something fast there is an involvement in protection against bad weather; and this protection 'is' for the sake of providing shelter."[17] Note here as well how subordinate purposes (e.g., connecting pieces of wood) serve larger purposes (e.g., providing shelter). The tool, then, serves a specific function—its in-order-to structure—for the sake of some larger purpose, and Heidegger notes that "the 'for-the-sake-of' always pertains to the being of [persons]."[18] The being of tools always and necessarily refers back to some human context.

WORLDS, FAMILIARITY, AND INVISIBILITY

Heidegger uses the term "world" in various ways.[19] For our purposes, we will use the term "world" to refer to a totality of significance, where

> Significance is not a category of things, one which gathers together into a separate domain certain objects with content in contrast to other kinds of objects and demarcates them over against another region of objects. It is rather a how of being, and indeed the categorical dimension of the being-there of the world

is centered in it. . . . This world is something being encountered as what we are concerned about and attend to.[20]

In other words, a world is circumscribed by the tools and know-how needed for us to move about effectively in that world.

Returning to tools, consider that a hammer is a hammer only in a world where it serves its function. In a world devoid of hammering, the hammer would not be a hammer at all and would merely be a wooden rod with a metal blob on one end. The being of the hammer is what it is because it belongs to a referential whole of work and know-how. In Heidegger's words, tools are "encountered always within an equipmental contexture. Each single piece of equipment carries this contexture along with it, and it is this tool only with regard to that contexture . . . . Equipmental character is constituted by what we call functionality."[21] And this functionality means that, as Dreyfus explains, "Equipment must fit into the context of meaningful activity . . . . Equipment makes sense only in the context of other equipment; our use of equipment makes sense because our activity has a point."[22] A tool "is what it is only insofar as it refers to other equipment and fits in a certain way into an 'equipmental whole'"[23] and "is defined by its function (in-order-to) in [that] referential whole."[24]

Tools, then, exist in specific equipmental contexts—*worlds*—such as the world of carpentry or the world of law.[25] A world circumscribes a specific set of tools and know-how, and a tool is understood in light of the role it plays in that world.[26] Tools are thus always world-dependent, and a tool can never exist in a vacuum. But, of course, tools are not restricted to conventional workshops. As an attorney, I inhabit the world of law, for which judicial decisions and computers are essential tools. I also inhabit this modern world, in which money and online account passwords are essential tools. Every world thus implies its own toolset and distinct know-how. These worlds are evolving and dynamic, and they can overlap with other worlds. The world of carpentry and metalwork, for example, overlap in some of the tools they employ, but they are not coextensive.

Because of this, we do not encounter the tools around us as mere things. For example, when we come upon the keyboard at our desk, we do not first see its dimensions or material composition. This is because the keyboard is not a mere thing, and the primary way we interface with things is, in Heidegger's words, "not a bare perceptual cognition, but rather that kind of concern which manipulates things and puts them to use."[27] To look at something as a mere thing, we must first de-world it, that is, take it out of the ontological world and place it in the ontic one, for example, by taking the hammer out of the world of hammering and seeing it "scientifically" by weighing it and measuring it.[28] Or, as in the example of happening upon a hammer in a world where there is no hammering, we might look at something as a mere thing when we come upon something that does not belong in our world such that we are forced to step back and look at it inquiringly. To know a tool, then, we cannot simply accumulate facts about it from detached study; we must actually use it. As Dreyfus explains, because a tool is what it is "in a context of use, i.e., how it is used in order to accomplish something, our most basic way of understanding equipment is to use it."[29] In Heidegger's words, "the *what-for* of [a tool's] usability is discovered along with the work itself."[30]

Thus, when the carpenter uses a hammer in their workshop, they don't see a wooden rod with a metal blob at the end; they simply use the hammer. And as we go about the work of our everyday lives, we do not see and interact with mere things; we employ tools. But neither is our attention during everyday experience focused on the tools themselves. "On the contrary, that with which we concern ourselves primarily is the work . . . . The work bears with it that referential totality within which the equipment is encountered."[31] In other words, as we approach our keyboard, we do not see a mere thing with certain properties, and we do not even really see our keyboard at all; instead, we just sit down and get to work, and the keyboard is there like it always is.

This experience, that of moving through a world in which we are at home, Heidegger calls familiarity. But we are always already in a world,[32] and so, in William Blattner's words, "our fundamental experience of the world is one of familiarity. We do not normally experience ourselves as subjects standing over against an object, but rather as at home in a world we already understand."[33] Thus, as we engage the tools of our world—all the things that are useful in one way or another—we usually do so in familiarity with what they are in relation to what they do within their respective worlds. This familiarity comes as a result of accumulated know-how. As we master the tools we need to move about our world, we need to think about them less and less, and we can instead simply focus on the work. This is why, according to Heidegger, "things constantly step back into the referential totality or, more properly stated, in the immediacy of everyday occupation they never even first step out of."[34] And here we arrive at one of Heidegger's other key insights: tools recede into the background of experience and become invisible when working properly within a familiar context.

If I am a carpenter, working in my shop, immersed in my work, when I reach for the hammer, I am likely not seeing the hammer at all. I am simply immersed in my work. I reach for the hammer. I use the hammer. I put it back. I do not see it because I am so familiar with it. As I type this, I have used the spacebar many times without being aware of its being there. The spacebar has effectively disappeared because it is there when I need it. It does what it is supposed to do. And this invisibility frees me to be fully engaged in the work of typing.

This invisibility is contingent on the tools performing as intended within a familiar world, however, and if there is a breakdown in this flow, if the tool fails to perform as it is supposed to, or if we find ourselves in an unfamiliar context, the usually invisible tool becomes visible.

> When a thing in the world around us becomes unusable, it becomes *conspicuous*. . . . The continuity of reference and thus the referential totality undergoes a distinctive disturbance which forces us to pause. When a tool is damaged and useless, its defect actually causes it to be present, conspicuous, so that it now forces itself into the foreground of the environing world in an emphatic sense. . . . The disturbance is . . . *a break in the familiar totality of references.*[35]

We can see the tool's bare in-order-to structure precisely because it fails to perform that specific function.[36] The spacebar's function as in-order-to-insert-one-space becomes conspicuous, for example, if it does not work (e.g., if it gives me two spaces instead of one), if it is missing (e.g., if my daughter plucked it off), or if I am looking for it on an unfamiliar keyboard (e.g., a keyboard designed for a language with which I am not familiar). Similarly, the hammer's specific function as in-order-to-strike becomes conspicuous if it is damaged, and I am now looking for something else to drive this nail back into the floorboard.

Note how unfamiliarity may arise when a tool is removed from its usual contexture. In a world devoid of hammering, the hammer would be unfamiliar, strange, and would thus present itself to us as an odd thing, and only because of this would its mere facts become salient. In Heidegger's words, something unfamiliar "stands in the way, comes at an inconvenient time, is uncomfortable, disturbing, awkward, hindering. As such, it has . . . a heightened 'there.'"[37] When we come across something "strange," "the question 'what is it' explicates itself into a 'What is it for? What are we supposed to do with it? Who is it for? What is it supposed to be? Who made it?'"[38] By the same token, a carpenter coming upon a rounding hammer, for example, would recognize the hammer as a hammer, but unless they know about its peculiar use in bookbinding, she would lack the context to understand it truly, and she would find herself wondering what it is and what it is for.

Note the world-dependent nature of ontological realities. Whereas the being of the rounding hammer qua mere thing is independent of human context (e.g., its material composition would remain constant regardless of who picks it up), its being qua tool is entirely dependent on its place in a particular world (e.g., the rounding hammer is unrecognizable as such to the carpenter). As Heidegger puts it, "[e]very entity that we uncover as equipment has with it a specific functionality"[39] and is thus, as Dreyfus explains, "defined in terms of what one uses it for."⁴⁰ Similarly, returning to the ontological reality of my fatherhood, whereas the statement "I have reproduced" points to a mere fact independent of human context, the statement "I am a father" is entirely world-dependent: the meaning of fatherhood and whether I qualify as a father will depend entirely on the context in which I find myself, and the meaning of fatherhood will shift between times and places.

This concealment through familiarity is even more apparent when considering more mundane examples. At home, we begin our day, we use the toilet, we brush our teeth, we get dressed, we go to work, we stop by the grocery store on the way home, we wind down, we go to sleep, we begin the cycle anew. We use myriad tools throughout the day every day, and these tools recede into the inconspicuous background of everyday experience as long as these are tools we have mastered and as long as we are using them in a familiar environment. We do not consider the toilet or our toothbrush or the cashier at the grocery store before availing ourselves of their functions. They are simply there as they always are for us to use so our conscious experience can be focused on the more important things of the day. But if there is a breakdown anywhere, the usually inconspicuous tool becomes highly conspicuous; it becomes obtrusive in the foreground of our consciousness, often in a frustrating manner because tools that should be operating in the background so we can go about our lives now stand out in their failure to perform their function and demand our attention.

At home, the toilet seat that should be in the background of my day becomes frustratingly foregrounded if it is dirty, or broken, or left up. At work, if my email is buggy or the formatting of a document is buggy, something that should be invisible becomes visible in the most unpleasant way. And when I stop by the grocery store after work to pick up a few things on my way home, the particular cashier that checks me out is part of the inconspicuous background experience of my day until I happen to be standing in line with a cashier in training and their role as an in-order-to-efficiently-charge-me-for-my-groceries becomes highly conspicuous in their failure to do so. But tools fade into the background only within a familiar context. When I wake up in a new place while traveling, a perfectly fine toilet seat may well be foregrounded in my conscious experience if it is a different shape than I am used to, for example. If I go to a grocery store that is unfamiliar to me, the background processes of pushing my shopping cart and retrieving items becomes foregrounded as I look for where things are in this particular store.

I once was at Best Buy looking for an HDMI cable. I was standing in an aisle, immersed in a comparison of two possibilities, trying to figure out which cable would be better suited to my needs, when I heard an "Excuse me?" When I turned around, this person said, "Can you help me? I want to buy a TV." I was confused, and my confusion must have registered because their face changed to confusion as well. I said, "I'm sorry. I don't work here." They apologized, but the way they did so told me they did not entirely believe me. It was not until I was back in the car and looked in the rearview mirror that I noticed I was wearing a polo shirt in a distinctive shade of Best Buy blue. As I had stood in that aisle, I was unwittingly wearing the uniform of a Best Buy employee. For their part, the person I interacted with was immersed in their own experience, their conscious mind occupied with the business of selecting the proper TV, and when they reached for the familiar tool of a uniformed employee, what was supposed to be part of the background of their day became foregrounded when a strange person wearing a Best Buy uniform claimed not to work there.

My Best Buy shirt served as a sign that I performed a particular type of function and was available as a particular type of tool. Those uniforms in a familiar context fade into the background and all the people wearing them are simply fungible uniformed employees until something fails and they become foregrounded. In the workplace, many persons in support roles operate, among other things, as sophisticated toolboxes. These roles perform a broad array of functions that support the parts of others' conscious experience, and often persons in these roles are most valued for being most inconspicuous, for fading into the invisible background of tools that make it so the people they support can go about their business without giving them a second thought. But that can only happen within a familiar environment where the person in the support role knows and performs their functions as expected. An untrained employee, by contrast, occupies the foreground of conscious experience until they can be trusted to perform their tasks as expected without supervision.

In this book, I focus on the phenomenon of persons as tools. The employment of human tools entails an interpersonal relation that is not at issue with nonhuman tools. The toilet seat does not care about my animus as I use it. It is different for the cashier or the Best Buy employee or the server staff at a banquet. A toilet seat is a tool, and a tool that fails to perform its function has no value. A cashier, despite serving the role of sophisticated toolbox, is primarily a person, someone who happens to work as a cashier and has value independent of their instrumental value. But as we go about our busy lives, we often do not stop and engage the person who happens to be performing a supporting role primarily as a person. Instead, persons performing supporting roles in our everyday lives simply fade into the background, and we engage with them qua tool, not qua person. The cashier, the mail carrier, the janitor, and the server at a banquet are each invaluable persons, but their personhood is not usually foregrounded in our experience. Instead, if they perform their roles well, they fade into the background, and if they fail to perform their roles properly, they are thrust into the foreground qua obtrusive tool failing to perform their function.

Consider servers at a banquet. If you are at a function where there are servers carrying trays of hors d'oeuvres and picking up used dishes, chances are these persons performing these roles will simply be part of the inconspicuous background of the event itself. But this would not be the case if one of them were just sitting there eating and drinking and having a great time. Worse yet, if you asked for help and they did not provide it, they would become highly conspicuous in their failure to perform their role as an in-order-to-serve. This phenomenon of visibility and invisibility of tools is critical when we consider persons as tools because the person performing a supporting role is invisible when performing that role well and visible when not performing that role well—but visible as a failing tool, not as a person—such that *what* function a person serves overtakes *who* the person is; the person is never seen as such. At the banquet, the persons performing the role of servers are reduced simply to *the servers*, and the persons behind those roles are never seen.

NOTES

1. Martin Heidegger, "The Question Concerning Technology," in *Basic Writings: From Being and Time (1927) to the Task of Thinking (1964)*, ed. David Farrell Krell (New York: Harper Collins Publishers Inc., 1993), 307.

2. Martin Heidegger, *Being and Time* (trans. John MacQuarrie and Edward Robinson) (New York: Harper Perennial, 1962). I will rely heavily on work by Hubert Dreyfus to explicate Heideggerian ontology. E.g., Hubert Dreyfus, *Being-in-the-World: A Commentary on Heidegger's Being and Time, Division I* (Cambridge: MIT Press, 1991).

3. Heidegger uses the term *vorhandenheit*. E.g., Heidegger, *Being and Time*, 48. It is tempting to translate this concept as referring to "objects" or, as Joan Stambaugh does in one instance, as "objective presence." Martin Heidegger, *Being and Time* (trans Joan Stambaugh) (Albany: SUNY Press, 2010), 6 n*. Stambaugh clarifies, however, that "'vorhanden' does not necessarily imply that that it has the character of being an 'object' or something 'objective'..., this qualification is especially important because it is always necessary to distinguish Dasein [the person] from anything like a subject." 6 n*. Any implication of a subject-object relation would undermine Heidegger's project to dissolve precisely this distinction. Martin Heidegger, *Ontology—The Hermeneutics of Facticity*, trans. John van Buren (Blomington: Indiana University Press, 1999), 62 ("This schema must be avoided: what exists are subjects and objects, consciousness and being"). To avoid these pitfalls in connotation, other translators opt for "occurrentness" (Dreyfus, *Being-in-the-World*, xi) or "presence-at-hand" (MacQuarrie and Robinson, 48 n.1). For purposes of this discussion, however, we will attempt to avoid this cumbersome jargon by referring to the being of "mere things." Cf. Heidegger, *Being and Time*, 97.

4. Dreyfus, *Being-in-the-World*, 84, 121.

5. In Dreyfus' explanation, the ontic view concerns facts about beings whereas the ontological view concerns ways of being. Dreyfus, *Being-in-the-World*, 19–21. I will generally follow this approach, and will reserve the term "ontological" exclusively for human dimensions.

6. Heidegger, *Being and Time*, 82 (persons "are present-at-hand 'in' the world, or, more exactly, *can* with some right and within certain limits be *taken* as merely present-at-hand. To do this, one must completely disregard or just not see the existential state of Being-in"). Italics in original.

7. Heidegger's term for "person" is *Dasein*, "an entity... distinguished by the fact that, in its very being, that being is an issue for it." Heidegger, *Being and Time*, 32.

8. Heidegger, *Being and Time*, 67. Unlike classical ontological approaches which attempted to create a taxonomy of being by looking at the components of a thing (e.g., whereas a chair is made of wood and nails, a person is made of body and soul), Heidegger proposes that "[w]e cannot define [a person's] essence by citing a 'what' of the kind that pertains to a subject matter,... its essence lies rather in the fact that in each case it has its being to be." Heidegger, *Being and Time*, 32–33.

9. Dreyfus, *Being-in-the-World*, 40 ("Heidegger calls the activity of existing, 'being-in-the-world.'"). Heidegger distinguishes the way persons are in the world (*In-der-Welt-sein*) from the spatial way mere things are in the world: "Being as in-being... does not signify anything spatial at all but means primarily being familiar with." Martin Heidegger, *History of the Concept of Time: Prolegomena* (trans Theodore Kisiel) (Bloomington: Indiana University Press, 1985), 158.

10. Heidegger, *History of the Concept of Time*, 153–154 ("The specification 'to be' the being directs us to understand all phenomena of Dasein primarily as ways of its 'to be.'").

11. Dreyfus, *Being-in-the-World*, 24–25 (discussing the distinction between factuality and facticity).

12. Heidegger, *Being and Time*, 68. Heidegger uses the term *zeug* to refer to tools. This term has been variously translated as "equipment" (MacQuarrie) or "useful things" (Stambaugh), for example. We will refer to "tools" to avoid the detached or stilted feel of the alternatives. Heidegger uses the term *zuhandenheit* to refer to the being of tools. This neologism has been variously translated as "ready to hand" (MacQuarrie), or "handiness" (Dreyfus, Stambaugh), for example. I will simply refer to "the being of tools."

13. Heidegger, *History of the Concept of Time*, 191; Heidegger, *Being and Time*, 97 ("Equipment is essentially 'something in-order-to.'").

14. Sara Ahmed, *Queer Phenomenology: Orientations, Objects, Others* (Durham: Duke University Press, 2006), 45.

15. Heidegger, *Being and Time*, 97.

16. Heidegger, *Being and Time*, 97, emphasis in original; Ahmed, *Queer Phenomenology*, 46.

17. Heidegger, *Being and Time*, 116–117.

18. Heidegger, *Being and Time*, 116–117.

19. Heidegger, *Being and Time*, 93; Dreyfus, *Being-in-the-World*, 89–91; William Blattner, *Heidegger's Being and Time: A Reader's Guide* (London: Bloomsbury, 2006), 43.

20. Heidegger, *Ontology*, 66.
21. Martin Heidegger, *The Basic Problems of Phenomenology*, trans. Albert Hofstadter (Bloomington: Indiana University Press, 1982), 292 (translating *Bewandtnis* as "functionality").
22. Dreyfus, *Being-in-the-World*, 91–92.
23. Dreyfus, *Being-in-the-World*, 62.
24. Dreyfus, *Being-in-the-World*, 91.
25. Heidegger, *Basic Problems of Phenomenology*, 165 ("We always understand world in holding ourselves in a contexture of functionality").
26. Heidegger, *History of the Concept of Time*, 192 ("The work-world is defined in the work."); Ahmed, *Queer Phenomenology*, 30 (discussing the family home as a world).
27. Heidegger, Being and Time, 95; Heidegger, Basic Problems of Phenomenology, 163.
28. Cf. Graham Harman, *Tool Being: Heidegger and the Metaphysics of Objects* (Chicago: Open Court, 2002), 22 (contrasting the "ontic" and the "ontological" view of the same tool).
29. Dreyfus, *Being-in-the-World*, 64.
30. Heidegger, *History of the Concept of Time*, 192; Heidegger, *Basic Problems of Phenomenology*, 304 ("Original familiarity with beings lies in dealing with them appropriately."). As Dreyfus explains, a tool "is what it is only insofar as it refers to other equipment and fits in a certain way into an 'equipmental whole.'" Dreyfus, *Being-in-the-World*, 62. "[E]quipment is defined by its function (in-order-to) in a referential whole." *Being-in-the-World*, 91. Tools are thus "encountered always within an equipmental contexture. Each single piece of equipment carries this contexture along with it, and it is this tool only with regard to that contexture.... Equipmental character is constituted by what we call functionality [*Bewandtnis*]." Heidegger, *Basic Problems of Phenomenology*, 292. Further, "to actually function, equipment must fit into the context of meaningful activity.... Equipment makes sense only in the context of other equipment; our use of equipment makes sense because our activity has a point." Dreyfus, *Being-in-the-World*, 91–92.
31. Heidegger, *Being and Time*, 99.
32. Heidegger, *Being and Time*, 120–121.
33. Blattner, *Heidegger's Being and Time* 12; 41–42 ("[W]e are *being-in-the-world*. Heidegger describes being-in-the-world as our basic state or constitution. The "being-in" or "inhood" that constitutes being-in-the-world is neither consciousness nor moral accountability but rather *familiarity* (*Vertrauheit*).").
34. Heidegger, *History of the Concept of Time*, 187; 152 ("What constantly conceals the phenomenal context to be laid open in this entity [Dasein] is the mistaking and misinterpreting indigenous to our intimate familiarity with that entity.")
35. Heidegger, *History of the Concept of Time*, 188. Tools are defined by their "functional roles in human life.... This understanding of equipment is most obvious when someone misuses the equipment." Blattner, *Heidegger's Being and Time*, 19.
36. Ahmed, *Queer Phenomenology*, 48.

37. Heidegger, *Ontology*, 77.
38. Heidegger, *Ontology*, 72; Heidegger, *History of the Concept of Time*, 191 ("The narrower the sphere of use, the more unequivocal the reference.").
39. Heidegger, *Basic Problems of Phenomenology*, 164.
40. Dreyfus, *Being-in-the-World*, 63.

Chapter 2

Ontological Brands

Tools have a specific function for the sake of some larger purpose within a particular world. Every tool exists within a referential whole of work and know-how. By the same token, every world implies particular work and requires unique know-how and a distinct toolset. Because we are always already in a world, our everyday experience is primarily one of familiarity. And because tools recede into the background of experience when they are working properly within a familiar context, the tools we encounter in our everyday dealings are largely invisible. These invisible tools become visible, however, when they fail to perform as they are supposed to or when we encounter them in an unfamiliar context.

Brands, such as those used on cattle or criminals, are tools. The brand is a sign[1] that transforms an invisible fact—e.g., that this particular cow belongs to that particular ranch—into one that is permanently visible, thereby introducing permanent distinctions among otherwise indistinguishable entities.[2] When cattle are branded, a branding iron is used to make an indelible mark on the animal. Both the branding iron and the brand itself are tools. The branding iron is an in-order-to-brand, the brand itself is an in-order-to-designate-as, and the branding is done for the sake of allowing us to see which animal belongs to which ranch within the particular world of ranching where these designations are recognized and respected. Note that the work of branding is necessary only because we begin with a field of animals that are otherwise indistinguishable.

The structure is similar to brands used on criminals. When a criminal is branded, a branding iron is used to make an indelible mark on the person, where the brand acts as an in-order-to-designate-as-criminal for the sake of punishment within a particular world where certain crimes are recognized and punished in that manner. The criminal brand is a sign that transforms an invisible fact—that this person has been convicted of a crime—into one that is permanently visible. But this works as punishment only because, unlike the cattle brand, the criminal brand carries profound ontological consequences. From the perspective of the cow, after all, other than the physical pain of being branded, there is no real change to the world. The cow's way of being in the world will be unaltered, and the cow will still go about its cow business unencumbered by the brand. The brand becomes just one more mere fact we can add to the pile of facts we can collect about this particular cow. And this, of course, is the case because, strictly speaking, the cow has no perspective, world, or being in the world. Persons do, however, and this is why criminal brands have an ontological impact. Besides the physical pain of being branded, the person is thrown into a different world after being branded a criminal, one in which they have been transformed from someone who has been convicted of a crime into someone who *is* a criminal.

Without a brand, a person convicted of a crime would be indistinguishable from someone who had not, and such a person could pass through the world unencumbered as any normal, presumptively always law-abiding citizen. But the purpose of the brand is to make that impossible. Though little more than skin deep, the brand irrevocably transmogrifies the bearer from a person simpliciter into a different kind of thing, into something shameful, something to be treated as other, as less than. The criminal brand thus serves as a permanent encumbrance to full access to the world, functioning as a stigma, explained in Erving Goffman's classic formulation as "an attribute that makes [someone] different from others in the category of persons available for him to be, and of a less desirable kind—in the extreme, a person who is quite thoroughly bad, or dangerous, or weak. He is thus reduced in our minds from a whole and usual person to a tainted, discounted one."[3]

The criminal brand not only makes visible an otherwise invisible fact, i.e., that this person has been convicted of a crime; the brand also transforms this invisible fact into visible ontological reality, i.e., that this person *is* a criminal. The brand renders the bearers criminals in se and thereby damns them to irredeemably demoted ontological status. The criminal brand designates-as-criminal, then, for the sake of punishment, but this punishment is inextricable from the larger purpose of establishing and policing distinctions between ordinary and disgraced members of society in a world where such distinctions matter deeply.[4]

Further, it is not merely that the person branded as a criminal would then be seen as such by the unbranded; the branded would not be able to avoid seeing their own brand. A new world is thus created by the act of branding, one in which the unbranded see *a criminal* and treat them as such, and in which the branded see their brand and see themselves seen and treated as a criminal. This results in cleavage in reality, in creation and splitting of worlds: whereas before the branding, there was no such thing as the branded and unbranded, whereas before the branding, all persons were—ceteris paribus—on equal ontological footing as persons simpliciter, after the branding, the branded live in a shrunken space, restricted in the category of persons available for them to be. The person branded as a criminal thus becomes a different type of entity. In that new world, the branded *is* a criminal, and that state of being enjoys inferior access to the opportunities of the world. The criminally branded would thus have no choice but to make their way through that new world by developing a distinct toolset and know-how for dealing with that new reality. In effect, the person branded as a criminal would end up having to create a new world crafting a distinct way of being in the world.

This is the ontological dimension of human branding. It is a system of tools used to manufacture disparate ontological realities. Ontological branding exists to transform the branded into ontologically demoted entities who only get to enjoy limited access to a world made by and for the unbranded. This is the crux of subordination through ontological power, i.e., the power to determine who gets to be a person simpliciter and who does not.[5] Ontological brands allow us to look at a person and make an immediate assessment as to their ontological status. This is the equivalent of simultaneously demanding and receiving a person's ontological papers. Like the badges employed by the Nazis, like a criminal brand on someone's face, ontological brands work precisely because they are visible signs generally recognized within their world. The system of ontological brandedness exists to create ontological privilege, the privilege enjoyed by the unbranded to count as a person simpliciter in a world where persons (and only persons) are equal and where persons simpliciter can expect demoted persons to serve roles that support that world.[6] The subtle and powerful privilege of unbrandedness—getting to count as a person in a world where only persons really matter—is the endgame of ontological branding, where the ontological privilege each of us enjoys is a measure of our respective distance from full personhood.

While the focus of this project is the modeling of race as an ontological brand, ontological brandedness theory may well be useful in modeling the mechanics of oppression in other spheres, particularly with regard to gender, queerness, and class. Each of these dimensions shares a common experience of restricted ways of being (allowed to be) in the (unbranded) world.[7] Each of these dimensions of subordination shares a story of struggle against ontological dominance.[8]

RACE AS ONTOLOGICAL BRAND

In the contemporary United States, the conventional understanding is that race is a fact that tells us something about the type of thing we are. Race may be a biological fact (e.g., whiteness and blackness correspond to particular constellations of phenotypic traits), a social fact (e.g., whiteness and blackness correspond to labels imposed by society given the particular norms operating at a particular place and time), or a combination of the two (e.g., whiteness and blackness correspond to constellations of phenotypic traits, but their meaning is socially constructed), but, regardless, race concerns the type of thing we are (e.g., a white person as opposed to a Black person). But I will argue that race is best understood as a brand that designates persons of color as ontologically demoted in order to privilege whiteness as the state of being of a person simpliciter in a world where all (and only) persons are equal. Race is thus a tool, specifically, race is an in-order-to-distinguish between who gets to count as a person simpliciter and who does not.

The tool of race is used to manufacture ontological privilege for the unbranded (i.e., white persons), namely, the privilege of getting to be one among a group of equals, each of whom is inherently and infinitely valuable as an individual. This privilege affords the unbranded nearly limitless access to ways of being in a world made by and for the unbranded. By the same token, those branded by race (i.e., persons of color) are excluded from full participation in that world and are instead relegated to playing subordinate roles in service to that world. By being excluded from the group of persons who are intrinsically valuable ends in themselves, persons of color become only instrumentally valuable inasmuch as they serve the interests of the white world that branded them. This ontological subordination limits a person of color's access to ways of being in the world. In the way that the criminal brand encumbers the person branded as criminal in their attempts to move freely through the (default) world, the brand of nonwhiteness encumbers persons of color in their attempts to move freely through the (white) world.

Race, as we know it today, is the result of a historical process that equated personhood with European identity. Through this process, whiteness became the mode of being of a person simpliciter, while those marked by nonwhiteness were demoted to an inferior ontological rank and properly destined for exploitation. This dynamic played out as liberalism and colonialism developed in tandem and resulted in a (white) world wherein European powers could see themselves as increasingly enlightened even as they sought to subjugate much of humanity. This same dynamic has played out in the history of American law, where the ontological brand of race was created by law and continues to be protected by law in the contemporary United States.

More particularly, in the United States, the brand of blackness was created to designate certain persons as tools themselves, as demoted persons properly restricted to roles in support of the (white) world. When Black persons have recognized their proper place and stayed in it, they have had a chance at fading into the inconspicuous background of (white) American life. When, however,

Black persons have moved beyond those confines, they have become highly conspicuous and invited the punishing gaze of the white world. While the fundamental distinction remains one between brandedness and unbrandedness, between whiteness and nonwhiteness in the racial context, it is important to underscore the primordial place of blackness within white supremacy. While all persons of color are ontologically demoted and constrained within (white) America, historically and presently, groups excluded from whiteness have been able to court favor with (white) America by joining in antiblack racism. In this book, I thus focus on the phenomenon of the brand of blackness while noting that the ontological machinery of white supremacy can, in many ways, extend to nonwhiteness generally.

Like the criminal brand, the brand of nonwhiteness serves as a sign to the world that a person of color is ontologically demoted, and it also has an existential bearing on the branded because they cannot but see themselves as branded in a world made by and for the unbranded. As a result, in the United States, the experience of nonwhiteness, in particular the experience of blackness, entails a complex system of operating within the shrunken space permitted branded persons within the unbranded world. This results in the creation of a world by and for the branded, a world with its distinct toolset and knowhow while whiteness, unbrandedness, enjoys its own privileged way of being in the (white) world.

GENDER AND BRANDEDNESS

In the terminology used here, we might think of gender as having ontic and ontological dimensions. Whereas the ontic might concern my biological role in reproduction, the ontological concerns my ways of being in the world.[9] The ontological dimensions of my gender are entirely world-dependent: I identify as a man, but what counts as manhood varies across times and cultures. Notably, men and women do not enjoy equal ontological status. Womanhood can be understood as a brand that marks women for ontological demotion, whereas manhood is unbranded, personhood simpliciter. The unbranded man thereby becomes not just a man, but *man*, the true and universal human form. This brand takes mere facts—e.g., certain secondary sex characteristics—and transforms these into an ontological reality—*womanhood*—for the sake of privileging manhood with personhood simpliciter in a world created by and for men.[10] Men can freely move through this patriarchal world unencumbered by gender, whereas women are restricted in their access to that world, encumbered by their feminized being.

In *Down Girl*, Kate Manne argues that "women will tend to face hostility of various kinds because they are women in a man's world," where the patriarchal order structuring this world should be "understood as one strand among various similar systems of domination (including racisms, xenophobia, classism, ageism, ableism, homophobia, transphobia, and so on)," and where misogyny operates as the "law enforcement branch" of the patriarchal order.[11] She argues that in this patriarchal world, the problem is not women as such but women who "violate or challenge the relevant norms or expectations."[12] In the language of ontological subordination adopted here, women are punished when they fail to operate within the confines of their ways of being *allowed to be* in the *man's* world.

Masculinity may be usefully modeled as ontological unbrandedness, i.e., as the state of personhood simpliciter, where gender may represent one dimension in which ontological power may be exerted to restrict a person's access to the privileges of full humanity by branding them as women, i.e., as ontologically demoted.[13] In this light, queerness may operate in a distinct but related dimension where queerness may be usefully modeled as an ontological brand that signals the not masculine, i.e., the ontologically demoted.[14] Thus, while the masculine (as expressed in cis men) may move unencumbered through the world by and for the unbranded, the not-masculine (queer cis men, trans men, nonbinary persons, women, etc.) are encumbered by a demoted ontological status.[15]

CLASS AND BRANDEDNESS

Because of its comparatively weak ontic substrate, socioeconomic class presents distinct challenges to modeling as an ontological brand. Nonetheless, a brandedness operant in class may be revealed with careful inspection. In class, a fact—a person's modest socioeconomic provenance—is transformed into ontological reality—that person *is* "lower class." Class can be understood as a branding system that demotes those designated as "lower class" to an inferior ontological status as compared with their unbranded, "upper class," counterparts. The "upper class" persons are thereby privileged with personhood simpliciter and thus given full access to the rights and privileges of the world (made by and for the unbranded).[16] Ontological power appears to operate in a class dimension, where those designated as "lower class" are ontologically demoted through mechanisms analogous to race and gender.[17] Despite our strong American belief in class mobility, it seems that "lower class"ness may best be modeled as an ontological brand, i.e., as something indelible, heritable, and apparent that serves to encumber the being in the world of the bearer of the "lower class" brand.

Considering Nancy Isenberg's *White Trash*, for example, "white trash"ness can be understood as an embodied identity.[18] Historically, "white trash"ness has comprised markers ranging from the physiological (e.g., the quality of skin or hair) to the cultural (e.g., mannerisms, speech patterns, clothing, and make-up), where these have served as signals of an inherent nature or identity.[19] The suggestion that class may operate as an ontological brand contradicts some of our most fundamental beliefs about class and the American ethos, but, as will be addressed further below, this reality is a direct result of our founding ideologies. Discussing America's founding on a rule of nature by which all men were understood to be created equal, Isenberg notes that this "rule of nature was supposed to supplant artificial aristocracy with meritocracy. At the same time, though, it allowed people to associate human failures with different strains and inferior breeds, and to assign a certain inevitability to such failure."[20]

INTERSECTIONALITY

Ontological branding creates a subtle and powerful privilege. It creates a group of unbranded people whose privilege is that very unbrandedness. To be branded is to be ontologically demoted, ineligible for participation in personhood simpliciter. In the United States, for example, the brand of blackness designates one as presumptively criminal. Women are branded as presumptively less competent. Coming from an economic underclass results in being branded as presumptively stupid. But if you are a white straight cis man from the right socioeconomic class, you are a fish in water. This world was designed by and for persons, i.e., those like you.

Under this model, privilege can be understood as a measure of one's distance from being a person simpliciter. The mathematics of oppression is one of subtraction: as will be developed below, brands work by marking some for fewer rights, not by marking some for more.[21] Brandedness theory may thus be useful in modeling the relationship between ontologically demoted groups. Because each brand operates as a distinct tool, each implies distinct ontological realities. A Black man and an Asian man, for example, share the common state of brandedness vis-à-vis whiteness while still representing distinct ontologies. A white man and a white woman share a common state of unbrandedness vis-à-vis race, but, vis-à-vis gender, the woman is branded while the man is unbranded. A white woman is branded, and a Black man unbranded, vis-à-vis gender; the white woman is unbranded, and the Black man branded, vis-à-vis race; and, in a way, they each experience both ontological privilege and ontological oppression, although of very different types, as they navigate through the various worlds they inhabit.

While all ontological brands exist for the sake of marking certain people for ontological demotion, each brand is distinct and irreducible to any other, where each brand implies its work, know-how, and even world.[22] All things being equal, a wealthy woman is more privileged than a poor woman because the poor woman is ontologically demoted in at least two distinct dimensions.[23] All things being equal, a white man is more privileged than a Black man because blackness brands one as ontologically demoted. But who is more privileged: a wealthy Black man or a poor white man? A white woman or a Black man? The ontological brandedness model provides no simple calculus by which comparative privilege can be weighed.[24] Instead, the value of ontological brandedness theory lies instead in illuminating how branding provides a distinct way of creating groups of people to oppress and illuminating how privilege is served by failing to see these categories as brands invented, imposed, and maintained. This model gives us a language to articulate the distinct experiences and consequences of being (allowed to be) in the world with our own complex of brandedness and/or unbrandedness.

Ontological brandedness theory thus provides a useful ontological framework for intersectional theory. As we approach the complex realities of intersectional identities, we can ask questions in terms of the distinct worlds created and maintained by the privileged—unbranded—status implied in each of these, and we can approach these as an exploration of distinct though interdependent worlds unfolding within an umbrella of a larger world made by and for the unbranded. Understanding the ontological oppression at play for a Black woman, for example, we can both consider blackness and womanhood as distinct brands with distinct genealogies and ontologies and, at the same time, recognize that blackwomanhood presents its own emergent ontology that is other than the simple sum of its parts.[25] Putting the focus on the ontological privilege conferred on unbrandedness discloses a system under which deviation from unbrandedness becomes abnormality, where there are manifold intersecting dimensions in which this deviation can play out and where, as Ladelle McWhorter puts it, "[w]e are different, but we live in the same world,"[26] i.e., the world by and for the unbranded; accordingly, "these things are joined together, part of the same matrix of power, employing the same means, serving the same aims, shaping the same lives."[27]

Brands are irreducible to one another (e.g., the "race problem" does not go away if we address the "class problem"), and brands combine to make emergent ontologies (e.g., the ontology of blackwomanhood is irreducible to the ontology of blackness plus the ontology of womanhood).[28] Additionally, complex power relations emerge when multiple dimensions of ontological oppression collide. Consider the interface between "white trash"ness and blackness, for example. While "white trash" may be "marked by class," whiteness still confers white privilege.[29] And, in fact, the very development of "white trash"ness has been essential to the development of white supremacy.[30]

Ultimately, because ontological branding exists for the sake of privileging unbrandedness with personhood simpliciter, policing the boundaries between brandedness and unbrandedness is essential for preserving the ontological privilege the unbranded enjoy. Thus, because a threat to unbrandedness anywhere is a threat to unbrandedness everywhere, it is not surprising that various systems of ontological oppression share common themes. A common theme emerges when looking at the historical relations between branded and unbranded groups: the branded are subject to restricted ways of being in the world, and when they challenge those confines, they experience backlash from the unbranded world.

NOTES

1. Heidegger addresses signs as an important type of tool whose purpose is "showing or indicating." Heidegger, *Being and Time*, 108; Heidegger, *History of the Concept of Time*, 204; Dreyfus, *Being-in-the-World*, 100.

2. "Ownership" is, of course, dependent on a human context in a way that the number of protons in a helium atom is not. We can think of these as mere facts, however, qua in-principle-verifiable—e.g., whether I own this particular cow is an in-principle verifiable fact with regards to which we can look at purchase receipts, for example. Whether the person doing the verification of this fact is here or in China, or does the verification today or tomorrow, the cow will or will not be mine as defined by the rules of ownership operant in that context.

3. Erving Goffman, *Stigma: Notes on the Management of Spoiled Identity* (New York: Simon & Schuster, 1986), 3. Scholarship on stigma is a field unto itself, and much has been developed since Goffman's groundbreaking work. E.g., Arthur Kleinman and Rachel Hall-Clifford, "Stigma: A Social, Cultural and Moral Process," 63 *Journal of Epidemiology & Community Health* 6 (2009).

4. For an analogous, present-day phenomenon, consider the stigma associated with having a criminal conviction on one's record and subsequent corrective attempts such as Ban the Box campaigns. See, e.g., Michelle Alexander, *The New Jim Crow: Mass Incarceration in the Age of Colorblindness* (New York: The New Press, 2010), 151; Austin, Regina, ""The Shame of It All": Stigma and the Political Disenfranchisement of Formerly Convicted and Incarcerated Persons," 36 *Colum. Hum. Rts. L. Rev.* 173 (2004) (exploring "the impact of the stigma of conviction and incarceration as experienced not only by minority offenders, but also by their families and communities, and the relationship of that stigma to political disenfranchisement."); Myisha Cherry, "State Racism, State Violence, and Vulnerable Solidarity," in *The Oxford Handbook on Philosophy and Race*, ed. Naomi Zack (Oxford: Oxford University Press, 2017).

5. Cf. Falguni A. Sheth, *Toward a Political Philosophy of Race* (New York: SUNY Press, 2009), 170 (discussing race in terms of "onto-power," that is, race as ontological category "assigned to populations under the auspices of a sovereign

authority that wields enough power to influence a widespread social discourse."). I will assume a distinction between ontology and metaphysics where ontology refers to world-dependent reality and metaphysics refers to something like a hypothetical god's-eye view. An ontological brand does not result in metaphysical inferiority. Ontological brandedness does nothing to alter the reality that "all human beings are morally equal and have equal intrinsic value." Naomi Zack, *White Privilege and Black Rights: The Injustice of U.S. Police Racial Profiling and Homicide* (Lanham: Rowman & Littlefield: 2015), 77 (discussing the liberalist credo of metaphysical equality among human beings). Metaphysically, a person remains a person, no matter what we do to them. Ontologically, however, the person branded receives a demotion and becomes subordinate for all intents and purposes within that world. While altering nothing metaphysically, in the world created by branding, the branded become subordinate beings who enjoy inferior access to that world, placed in what Catharine MacKinnon calls "a condition of imposed inferiority." Catherine A. MacKinnon, *Toward a Feminist Theory of the State* (Cambridge: Harvard University Press, 1989)241. See Robin Dembroff, "Real Talk on the Metaphysics of Gender," 46 *Philos. Topics* 2 (fall 2018): 23 (discussing ontological oppression when "social kinds (or the lack thereof) unjustly constrain (or enable) persons' behaviors, concepts, or affect due to their group membership.").

6. Cf. Ladelle McWhorter, *Racism and Sexual Oppression in Anglo-America: A Genealogy* (Indianapolis: Indiana University Press, 2009), 292 ("[R]acism looms much larger and goes much deeper in our national and in our personal lives than even the most racially aware and sensitive among us think. It structures all our educational institutions; it informs all our medical protocols; it shapes our self-perceptions as well as our perceptions of every person we meet. Our halls of justice reverberate with it. Our prisons and hospitals and asylums grow crowded with the consequences of it. Racism against the abnormal permeates virtually every aspect of contemporary life and is responsible for many of the disparities and injustices that mark our society.").

7. Manne, *Down Girl*, xiii; Ahmed, *Queer Phenomenology*, 136 (discussing whiteness as a necessary but not sufficient condition of privilege, where gender, sexual orientation, and class also come to bear); McWhorter, *Racism and Sexual Oppression in Anglo-America*, 319 (addressing a normality defined as "middle-class white masculinity and femininity as well as licensed monogamy."); Charles Mills, *Black Rights/ White Wrongs*, 122; Kendi, *Stamped from the Beginning*, 280 (discussing the "convergence of racist, sexist, and homophobic ideas"); MacKinnon, *Toward a Feminist Theory of the State*, 237 (gender "is lived as ontology, not epistemology").

8. MacKinnon, Toward a Feminist Theory of the State, 240.

9. See Linda Martín Alcoff, *Visible Identities: Race, Gender, and the Self* (Oxford: Oxford University Press, 2006).

10. Gender provides an interesting foil to race as it involves ontic differences lacking in race. As Alcoff puts it, "sexism has more to work with." Martín Alcoff, *Visible Identities*, 164. None of this changes the reality that while sex may be have ontic presence, no matter how robust, the ontological implications of being of a particular sex are determined by the reality that womanhood entails a subordinated brand within a patriarchal world.

11. Manne, *Down Girl*, 32; 13 ("Misogyny does this by visiting hostile or adverse social consequences on a certain (more or less circumscribed) class of girls or women to enforce and police social norms that are gendered either in theory (i.e., content) or in practice (i.e., norm enforcement mechanisms).")

12. Manne, *Down Girl*, 20.

13. Cf. Dembroff, "Real Talk on the Metaphysics of Gender."

14. Ahmed, *Queer Phenomenology*, 127 ("The prohibition of miscegenation and homosexuality belong, as it were, in the same register").

15. This phenomenon dovetails with the subordination of Black men branded as dangerously hypersexual and thus expected to tone down their masculinity in the presence of white persons. McWhorter, *Racism and Sexual Oppression in Anglo-America*.

16. The policing of the boundary between classes can perhaps be usefully modeled as the policing of an ontological boundary between the branded and the unbranded. See Nancy Isenberg, *White Trash: The 400-Year Untold History of Class in America* (New York: Viking, 2016).

17. See Isenberg, *White Trash*; Linda Martín Alcoff, *The Future of Whiteness* (Cambridge: Polity, 2015); George Yancy, *Black Bodies, White Gazes: The Continuing Significance of Race in America*, 2nd ed. (New York, Rowman & Littlefield: 2017), 18 (discussing the ways poor white persons were otherized).

18. Isenberg, *White Trash*, 315.

19. Consider, for example, that even someone like President Lyndon B. Johnson "knew in his heart that his place among the power elite was not really secured; he was not fully accepted. A country boy might at any moment reveal some telltale sign of a white trash character. He might say something inappropriate. He could never conceal the artless drawl or dust off the sticky red clay. Indelible marks of class identity were forever stamped on him, no matter how far he wandered from the inhospitable land of his birth." Isenberg, *White Trash*, 266.

20. Isenberg, *White Trash*, 316.

21. Cf. Yancy, *Black Bodies, White Gazes*, 159 (a slave is not a natural category, it needs a master; so too is superiority of whiteness predicated on the "inferiorization of Blackness.")

22. Cf. Mills, *Black Rights/ White Wrongs*, 120 (arguing that the fundamental problem with Marxist theory is its failure to recognize race as a system of domination in itself); Mills, *Racial Contract*, 59 (noting that racial privilege can persist despite lack of socioeconomic privilege); Yancy, *Black Bodies, White Gazes*, 88 (discussing how in social hierarchy the white woman is above the Black man and the Black man above the Black woman—the Black woman is "the furthest thing from human."); Martín Alcoff, *Visible Identities*; Isenberg, *White Trash*.

23. Cf. Kendi, *Stamped from the Beginning*, 281 (noting that white lesbians and Black heterosexual women are higher on the ontological scale than Black lesbians).

24. This does not assume white privilege means all whites are privileged in the colloquial sense of the word. Cf. Mills, *Black Rights/ White Wrongs*, 121.

25. Black men are ontologically privileged qua men, and, while it makes sense to speak of the brand of blackwomanhood as distinct from the brand of blackmanhood, the latter, while it is subject to multiple mechanisms of subordination, still enjoys

ontological privilege given that it unfolds within a patriarchal world. Cf. Yancy, *Black Bodies, White Gazes*, 29 (arguing that "there is no male qua male" because "Black maleness" carries its own ontological implications.).

26. McWhorter, *Racism and Sexual Oppression in Anglo-America*, 328.

27. McWhorter, *Racism and Sexual Oppression in Anglo-America*, 1, 34.

28. Cf. Devon W. Carbado and Cheryl I. Harris, "Intersectionality at 30: Mapping the Margins of Anti-Essentialism, Intersectionality, and Dominance Theory," 132 *Harv. L. Rev.* 2193 (2019).

29. Yancy, *Black Bodies, White Gazes*, 225.

30. Kendi, *Stamped from the Beginning*, 238.

Chapter 3

A Genealogy of (White) America

In the contemporary United States, race is best understood as a brand that designates persons of color as subordinate persons in order to privilege whiteness as the state of being of a person simpliciter. As Charles Mills puts it, race is a "marker of personhood and subpersonhood."[1] Because race is a tool and a familiar part of everyday American life, race operates in a way that is largely invisible to many of us. This has resulted in an America which formally operates with an understanding that all persons are equal and entitled to equal access to constitutional rights. However, it is also an America where only white persons truly count as persons and where persons of color have effectively been excluded from the "We" of the "We the people." This (white) America has become what it is through U.S. law. It was U.S. law that created race as we now understand it, and it is through U.S. law that persons of color, especially Black persons, have been subordinated for the sake of privileging whiteness. Despite dramatic legal changes since the days of slavery, U.S. law continues to safeguard the interests of white supremacy even as it professes to be colorblind.

While the ontological brandedness model of race I develop concerns the creation and preservation of a boundary between whiteness and nonwhiteness generally, in this work, I focus on blackness and antiblack racism in the United States. This focus is analytically useful because the boundaries between whiteness and blackness in America have been more stringently policed and studied than any other racial boundaries. However, this focus is also necessary because in the United States blackness has been and continues to be anchored as the quintessential racial other.[2] From the time of the Enlightenment, when Kant proclaimed it "self-evident" that white and black were the two "base races," to the present-day, when the leader of Senate Republicans distinguishes between "Americans" and "African Americans," the black-white binary continues as the foundation of white supremacy.³ The Black person in America, in the words of George Yancy, embodies "a Black body that is rendered ersatz and is, collectively, one that has fought mightily to be included within a (white) body politic that is governed by an ontology that has been deeply shaped by whiteness as the transcendental norm, leaving whiteness unmarked, unraced, and as the human simpliciter."⁴ As Cornel West succinctly put it, "[t]he notion that black people are human beings is a relatively new discovery in the modern West."⁵

It is important to note that where varying axes of oppression intersect, blackness and antiblack racism will operate with significant differences. Within a patriarchal world, for example, a Black man and a Black woman will not experience blackness and antiblack racism in the same way, nor will harm suffered (or solutions required) be identical. Nonetheless, because the brand of blackness is a ubiquitous tool within the (white) world, it carries a common meaning regardless of the bearer. I argue that antiblack racism in the United States has at its core the reduction of the Black person to a tool; the person branded with blackness is designated as an in-order-to-serve-(white)-America. Thus, while race operates principally to distinguish between whiteness and nonwhiteness in order to exclude nonwhite persons from full participation in the (white) world, the brand of blackness in the United States was created specifically to designate Black persons as entities devoid of intrinsic value and whose lives mattered only inasmuch as they served the interests of the white world. As I set forth below, the brand of blackness was created by and continues to be maintained through law.

What are we to make of other nonwhite groups? Certainly, the story of colonialism is the story of the West turning its gaze to the world and rendering the rest of humanity as resources to be exploited. And specifically, in the United States, Black persons are not the only racialized group to be exploited by (white) America. I argue that in the United States to be branded as nonwhite is to be excluded from full participation in all the rights and privileges enjoyed by a person simpliciter. Under this system, all persons of color are subject to exploitation and marginalization. But blackness retains its anchored position as the racial other. This is especially salient when considering antiblack racism within other nonwhite racialized groups.⁶

If all persons of color are branded as in-order-to-serve-(white)-America, what is the nature of the brand borne by other racialized groups? These are fundamental questions in need of additional work. As a Mexican immigrant, the question of American Latinidad is particularly close to me.⁷ Below I undertake a genealogy of white supremacy in the United States, which is inextricable from a genealogy of the brand of blackness. To explore questions of the ontology of American Latinidad or any other racialized group will require a similar genealogy to explore the development of the brand within the hegemony of American whiteness. However, despite nuances and differences, the common experience of persons of color within (white) America is one of exploitation, exclusion, and ontological constraint. By demoting persons branded as nonwhite and privileging whiteness, thereby, white people get to move freely as equals through a world made by and for them (with the important caveat that this equality is disrupted for those oppressed through other axes such as gender, queerness, disability, or class). In contrast, persons of color are excluded from full participation in that world and instead relegated to playing subordinate roles supporting that world. This ontological inequality corresponds to concrete inequalities evident in the differential treatment experienced by white and Black persons before our various legal and social institutions and the different existential realities white and Black persons face.[8]

To be white, that is, unbranded, is to be a person simpliciter in a world by and for persons. In ordinary everydayness, white Americans largely experience themselves as ordinary persons going about their ordinary lives, unraced and at home in the world.[9] By contrast, in America, as Yancy puts it, "it is difficult for Blacks to be 'just me'"[10] because a Black person is not allowed to *be* in the same ways a white person is allowed to be.[11] Instead, Black persons are permitted to participate in (white) America to the degree that they stay in their subordinate place and accept that Black lives do not matter as much as white ones. If a Black person stays in that permitted place, they play their allotted supporting role and recede into the invisible background of (white) America. But if a Black person challenges these confines and attempts to move beyond the role permitted them, they become obtrusive and invite punishment. For a Black person, race is an ever-present reminder of being branded, of being seen "through the revelation of the other [white] world" as subordinate based on a marked body.[12] This experience creates in the Black person an existential split that a white person does not need to face: as a branded person, the experience is one of your raced body preceding you in a white world, a world in which you are ever returned to yourself through the eyes of others as less than what you are, a world which is not yours, a world with which you can never be fully familiar, a world in which you will never truly be at home.[13]

Sara Ahmed's work on race and phenomenology is helpful at this juncture. Because ours is a "world orientated 'around' whiteness," Ahmed argues, "whiteness is an orientation that puts certain things within reach," and race becomes "a question of what is within reach, what is available to perceive and to do 'things' with."[14] In this world, "whiteness is invisible and unmarked, as the absent center against which others appear only as deviants or as a line of deviation."[15] Accordingly, white persons are "oriented" so that the things of this world are "within reach" for them, available to use.[16] The net result is that white persons will be "at home in a world that is orientated around whiteness,"[17] while nonwhite persons will instead "stand out" and be seen as (and feel) "out of place."[18] To be a person of color in the white world, then, is not to have full access to the things of the world, to find that the things of the world are always just out of reach. In this world, "the familiar world, the world of whiteness,"[19] whiteness becomes the "'starting point' of orientation. Whiteness becomes what is 'here,' a line from which the world unfolds, which also makes what is 'there' on 'the other side.'"[20] In a (white) world, then, whiteness is a familiar, normal, natural, and invisible home base; nonwhiteness, by contrast, becomes other, the strange, the abnormal, the unnatural, and the obtrusive. (White) America is a place always already occupied by whiteness; to be a person of color living in the United States is to live in occupied territory.

The brand of race operates by transforming mere facts—for example, *having* a constellation of phenotypic features—into ontological realities—that is, *being* a subordinate person in a visible, permanent, and heritable manner. This branding of certain persons as nonwhite results in the manufacture of ontological distinctions between persons who would be otherwise equal. Accordingly, as Yancy puts it, race is best approached "not in terms of an ontology of essences, but in terms of a historical ontology that appreciates the fluidity of the historical formation of the meaning of, in this case, the Black body and the white body."[21] This implies a distinction between particular brands (e.g., to be branded "Black" and to be branded "Asian" implies different ontologies), but the fundamental distinction becomes that between the unbranded and the branded, between a person simpliciter and one subordinate.[22] Persons of color are branded, that is, ontologically demoted, by race, and whiteness corresponds to the state of being unbranded, that is, ontologically privileged as a person simpliciter.[23] Race is thus about how we are (allowed to be) in the world.[24] Borrowing Catharine MacKinnon's analysis vis-à-vis gender, race "is more an inequality of power than a differentiation that is accurate or inaccurate."[25] Race is a power dynamic, and it is part of a system within which "[w]hiteness, as normative, deems itself unmarked, invisible, and transparent."[26] And herein lies the crux of ontological power as operant in the dimension of race. As Yancy puts it,

> [i]n diverging or deviating from whiteness (the "nonracial" center), the yellow, the black, and the red are signifiers of inferior difference compared to whiteness as the same/ transcendental norm . . . . [N]ot only does whiteness reserve the power to define others as "divergent" or "deviant" but it also has the power to define "differences" entirely outside the standard–divergence dialectic.[27]

Whiteness is thus the state of being ontologically unencumbered,[28] and nonwhiteness is encumbered by what MacKinnon has called "a condition of imposed inferiority."[29]

Historically and currently, directly by design and indirectly through self-interest, the American system of ontological brands has created laws, institutions, and cultural norms—a *world*—in which whiteness is privileged as the mode of being of personhood.[30] The result, in Ahmed's words, is that "[t]his is the familiar world, the world of whiteness, a world we know implicitly."[31] It is the nature of tools to recede into invisibility when used skillfully within a familiar context. Because Americans are always already in a world where persons of color are branded, our use of the tool of race is familiar and largely invisible, especially to white people who get to move freely and feel at home within this (white) world.[32]

This white supremacist world, the world of (white) America, is maintained and protected by our collective participation in the everyday work of racing, that is, the work of seeing brandedness and acting accordingly. But it is not the case that we see race and then make judgments based on this seeing, as if we were looking at a product's label at the grocery store before deciding whether it is worth a purchase. Instead, because this is a common tool we are always already using, we participate in the process of racing by seeing the brand and acting accordingly in a preconscious manner.[33] As with other tools rendered invisible by familiarity, however, race can be made conspicuous by exploring breakdown cases, that is, situations in which the tool fails to serve its intended purpose, thereby rendering it conspicuous.

In this chapter, I undertake a genealogy of (white) America to bring to light that which has become invisible through familiarity. This project intends to, as Foucault put it,

> show that laws deceive, that kings wear masks, that power creates illusions, and that historians tell lies. This will not, then, be a history of continuity, but a history of the deciphering, the detection of the secret, of the outwitting of the ruse, and of the reappropriation of a knowledge that has been distorted or buried. It will decipher a truth that has been sealed.[34]

THE BRANDING IRON: RECONCILING EQUALITY AND SUBORDINATION

Under the model I propose, whiteness is ontological unbrandedness vis-à-vis race. Whiteness is not a badge of superiority; it is simply the way of being of a person simpliciter, and race serves to designate persons of color as falling short of that standard of personhood. Whiteness is what remains when everyone else has been ontologically demoted through the brand of race. But how? If race is a brand, what is the branding iron? When and how does the branding happen?

The branding iron of race was forged by and for the tension between the Enlightenment and colonialism. By manufacturing ontological hierarchies to exclude the branded from full participation in personhood, the unbranded were free to create a world for themselves and consider it a world for all persons.[35] But this world did not only exclude the branded, it relegated the branded to subordinate roles supporting that very world.[36] Although race was fabricated, it became real because it corresponded to a real disparity in power between brandedness and unbrandedness. This system of ontological subordination through the brand of race perpetuates and protects the privileging of whiteness in a world made by and for whiteness. White supremacy emerged as the solution to the tension inherent between the Enlightenment and colonialism. Specifically in the United States, white supremacy was how to reconcile our egalitarian ideals with our barbaric reality of slavery and genocide. In the present day, while we have morphed from an explicitly racialized legal system to one that is largely colorblind, the underlying system of privileging whiteness by subordinating nonwhiteness has remained a constant throughout.

From the very beginnings of modernity, through the Enlightenment, and to the present day, the West has been winding its way down a road of increasing recognition of universal human equality. This journey—we in the Unites States like to think, at any rate—culminated in the founding of an exceptional society willing to recognize the self-evident truths that all men are created equal and endowed with the inalienable rights to life, liberty, and the pursuit of happiness. But at the same time the Enlightenment unfurled into the recognition that each and all persons are equal because each and all persons are infinitely valuable ends in themselves, colonialism went into full swing, predicated on the justifiable plunder, enslavement, rape, and/or extermination of the majority of humanity. This presented a significant ideological problem. Whereas humanity had certainly plundered, enslaved, raped, and exterminated before, never had power operated under the constraints of a purported belief in universal human equality.[37] A commitment to the Enlightenment demanded that colonial power be justified with reason.

In that tension between the Enlightenment and colonialism, the intellectual firepower of the day forged an ingenious solution, the "scientific racism" that provided a purportedly empirical basis for finding non-Europeans to be inferior beings and justifying, as Yancy puts it, the "assumption that whiteness signified humanity as such."[38] After all, if it turned out to be the case that only Europeans were fully human, the West could have its cake and eat it too: it could move forward in the Enlightenment and leave colonialism unencumbered because its atrocities were not atrocities at all; they were actions perpetrated on entities not owed full human rights and who were treated as they were out of necessity, often for their own good. And so it was that as the Western intellectual animus sought to shake off commitments to natural human hierarchies and divine rights of kings, as humanism professed the infinite and inviolable worth of every person, all were simultaneously advancing the project of global white supremacy.[39]

This apologist project culminated in a hierarchical understanding of the Great Chain of Being, where life could be understood in terms of increasing sophistication, from sponges to ducks to apes to persons, and, within the lattermost category, human beings could be categorized by their respective races, where these were themselves understood in hierarchical terms in keeping with the inherent order of the natural world.[40] As Charles Mills explains, given the "scientific" conclusion that, in Kant's own words, "Humanity exists in its greatest perfection in the white race,"[41] "a category crystallized over time in European thought to represent entities who are *humanoid* but not fully *human* . . . and who are identified as such by being members of the general set of nonwhite races."[42] Africans ended up being placed in the bottom of the humanoid hierarchy, but other nonwhite races also came to be branded as inferior.[43] Whereas in the ancient and medieval worlds "inequality was the norm, modernity was supposed to usher in the epoch when all humans were seen as, and treated as, equal rights-bearing persons."[44] But instead, *person* became "a technical term, a term of art," that excluded non-Europeans by branding them as "savages" and "barbarians."[45] Far from the universalist rhetoric, modernity was really about "bringing about white (male) equality while establishing nonwhite inequality as an accompanying norm."[46]

This nonwhite inequality had a particular purpose in mind: the reduction of non-European humanity to resources to be exploited. It is no coincidence, as James Michael Taylor notes, that technology, colonialism, and race arose together.[47] Technology, after all, was about the transformation of resources, raw material, into something useful. The West needed what Falguni Sheth has described as the technology of race to transform the raw material of non-European humanity into resources to be exploited—all without threatening the integrity of the Enlightenment's commitment to universal human equality.[48] As the Enlightenment developed an understanding of persons as intrinsically valuable ends in themselves, it also brought an approach to understanding the world in terms of its utility, looking at the natural world not as something intrinsically valuable but only instrumentally so. The nonhuman world was a vast reserve of resources to be conquered, mastered, and exploited. This meant that when non-European humanity was excluded from full participation in personhood, it was by the same stroke relegated to that universe of things available to be conquered, mastered, and exploited. The brand of race thus permitted Western colonialism to advance secure in its white supremacist foundation, all while maintaining an evolving façade of universal human freedom and equality.

Western man thus stepped onto the world stage, boldly moving past primitive beliefs in the inherent superiority of certain people and ready instead to found a new world order predicated on the egalitarianism of achievement through demonstrable merit. But simultaneously and as part of the same project, Western man divided humanity into those who counted as true persons and those who did not. If the value of the Western man inhered in his personhood and afforded him the natural right to be treated as such, the value of those branded by race was not intrinsic but instrumental, derived from their capacity to participate in the world the West was making according to the terms the West was setting.[49] It is thus no surprise that the Enlightenment would understand colonialism not as a contradiction but rather an expression of the same ideals. After all, wherever the West invaded, conquest, subjugation, and genocide were seen as liberating acts because they were bringing light into the heart of darkness.[50] "When men oppress their fellowmen," Kendi has observed, "the oppressor ever finds, in the character of the oppressed, a full justification for his oppression."[51] As Mills explains,

> The whole point of establishing a moral hierarchy and juridically partitioning the polity according to race is to secure and legitimate the privileging of those individuals designated as white/persons and the exploitation of those individuals designated as nonwhite/subpersons.[52]

The purportedly scientific approach to white supremacy was essential to the legitimacy of the American project as well as to Europe's mushrooming colonialism. How could the horrors of slavery, manifest destiny, colonial exploitation, and genocide be justified by a newly enlightened West if not for the fact that nonwhiteness served as the natural sign of a person's subordinate status in the chain of human being?[53] America was founded on the lofty liberalist principles that all men are created equal and endowed with inalienable rights, with the important caveat that non-Europeans—Africans in particular—were, as our own Supreme Court clarified at one point, "beings of an inferior order."[54]

This apparent paradox—consider the horrors of slavery unfolding alongside a revolutionary fervor for universal equality—dissolves if race is properly understood. In the mythological foundation of America, notions of congenital superiority were summarily rejected. There would be no place in this New World for nobility, no heritable titles, virtues, or badges of superiority. America was founded precisely against the notion that some persons were better suited for wielding power over others. But such a proscription on badges of superiority amongst persons can be observed without contradiction alongside slavery if the enslaved fall outside of the protected scope of personhood. This powerful formula, liberalism plus the ontological brand of race, yielded one inevitable result—a white supremacist state that saw itself as egalitarian.[55]

This dynamic is fruitfully illuminated by Mills' concept of a domination contract.[56] Under standard notions of an idealized social contract,[57] the "crucial metamorphosis" is from "natural" to "civil/political," where "'state of nature' supposedly indicates the condition of all men, and the social metamorphosis affects them all in the same way."[58] But, following Sarah Pateman's feminist work,[59] Mills argues that because the definition of personhood has been restricted to white people,[60] a better model would be a racial contract in which "Whites 'contract' to regard one another as moral equals who are superior to nonwhites and who create, accordingly, governments, legal systems, and economic structures that privilege them at the expense of people of color."[61] Within a domination contract, then, the crucial distinction is between who gets to count as a person and who does not.[62] As regards the racial contract, "the crucial metamorphosis is the preliminary conceptual partitioning and corresponding transformation of human populations into 'white' and 'nonwhite' men,"[63] where "the general purpose of the Contract is always the differential privileging of the whites as a group with respect to the nonwhites as a group."[64] Race thus "establishes a fundamental partition in the social ontology of the planet, which could be represented as the divide between persons and subpersons,"[65] where whiteness becomes the state of being of personhood simpliciter.[66] Whiteness was created *ex nihilo* by branding non-European humanity as inferior.[67]

The mechanics of ontological branding are analogous to the system of badges employed by the Nazi regime. In order to distinguish between those who would count as persons and those who would not, obligatory badges were issued so the bearers' ontological status would be readily apparent. There were no "normal person" badges. It was unnecessary. By clearly designating those excluded from personhood, the unbadged were free to move freely in that world. Race similarly operates negatively: by excluding some from full personhood, the benefits of whiteness become simply getting to be a person in a world made by and for persons. Whiteness is not a brand or badge of superiority; it is simply the mode of being of personhood.[68] This is written into the very myth and letter of our foundation. The hallowed declarations that "all men are created equal" and "we the people" are egalitarian precisely because they admit to no marks of superiority. By branding certain people as demoted, the unbranded could enjoy ontological superiority without ever challenging their mythology of egalitarianism. In the end, colonialism made a world in which whiteness, that is, unbrandedness, that is, the way normal personhood happens to be, was free to simply recede into what Heidegger called "the pale and inconspicuous presence of the world."[69]

Unlike the Nazi badge system, however, the creation of race and the subordination of nonwhiteness emerged not as the result of a specific political program. Instead, race came about as the result of an evolving system of power.[70] Without needing to posit a conspiracy of founding fathers, race can be understood to have emerged organically in the West in a way that conveniently justified the domination of most of humanity by relegating it to a caste of permanent inferiority, a necessary step for a society interested in maintaining both white supremacy and liberal democratic ideals. The devastating genius of the invention of race lay in its being apparent, permanent, and heritable. Unlike the brand of the criminal, the brand of race would pass on to children. Generations of people would be born, as Ibram Kendi puts it, "stamped from the beginning."[71]

The great epistemic triumph of scientific racism was the normalization of whiteness. Even as the West grew increasingly resistant to slavery in the 19th century, and even as it grew increasingly resistant to apartheid in the 20th, as Ladelle McWhorter notes, "the white race . . . was and is viewed by most people—white or not and consciously or not—as the normal race, and all other races were and are viewed as deviant with respect to it."[72] Michel Foucault's work on normalization is instructive in this regard, and it becomes evident how "[r]acism plays out . . . as a crusade against deviance, against the threat posed by abnormality or pathology."[73] As Foucault suggests at the end of *Abnormal*, racism can be understood as

> racism against the abnormal, against individuals who as carriers of a condition, stigmata, or any defect whatsoever, may more or less randomly transmit to their heirs the unpredictable consequences of the evil, or rather of the non-normal, that they carry within them.[74]

Over time, with whiteness firmly established as normality, Western ideologies of race came to be "preoccupied not with attacking members of another race but with protecting the boundaries of *the* race, the only race that matters, the human embodied in its 'highest' representatives."[75] These highest representatives, the unbranded, now enjoy a privileged existence by virtue of the fact that the branded are ontologically demoted, and the modern "racism against the abnormal" serves to police the foundational boundary between brandedness and unbrandedness.

THE BIRTH OF A (WHITE) NATION: CREATING AND USING THE BRAND OF BLACKNESS

The enslavement of 700,000 persons at the time the Bill of Rights was ratified and nearly four million by the time the opening shot was fired in the Civil War was possible under the American banner because persons branded with blackness were not considered persons at all. While European powers saw themselves as the lords of mankind, America was supposed to be different, "an egalitarian (if a bit flawed) liberal democracy free of the hierarchical social structures of the old world," as Mills puts it.[76] We in America are accustomed to thinking of ourselves as exceptional, and (white) America tends to see racism as an aberration, a departure from who we are. But systemic and institutionalized racial injustice is exactly what America was designed to be.[77] The white supremacist project of creating and subordinating blackness was necessary for the American project to operate in the liberalist zeitgeist within which it unfolded.[78] As James Baldwin succinctly put it, "The story of the Negro in America is the story of America. It is not a pretty story."[79]

But how did the distinctly American brand of blackness come to be? As the work of scholars such as Kendi and Jacqueline Jones reveals, race emerged as the solution to two significant problems. First, there was the theoretical problem of reconciling slavery with Enlightenment values that would blossom into a liberal democracy. But there was also the practical problem early colonists faced by maintaining a disparate labor force comprising enslaved persons from various African and indigenous groups as well as European indentured servants: the enslavement of indigenous persons carried the risk of antagonizing the local groups to whom they belonged, European indentured servants enjoyed a schedule of rights, at least formally, and there was a constant threat of the entire labor force organizing and revolting against the colonists.[80]

The brand of blackness was the tool that emerged to solve both of these problems. By imposing the same brand of ontological inferiority on all people of African descent, their enslavement fell outside the system of protections owed proper persons, thereby addressing the theoretical problem. Ideological coherence could be maintained by "considering these African people to be stamped from the beginning as a racially distinct people, as lower than themselves, and as lower in the scale of being than the more populous White indentured servants."[81] The brand of blackness solved the practical problem as well. In contrast to enslaved indigenous persons and English indentured servants, as Jones explains, "African captives had no advocate, no protector, in the New World, whether in the form of a well-armed nation-state or lawyers representing a traditional body of law. Thus, the English and other European groups felt free to exploit Africans and their descendants with impunity."[82] By the same token, the invention of Blackness and its subordination to whiteness would serve as a wedge between racial groups to neutralize the threat of a labor force organized across racial lines.[83]

The ontological violence wrought through the Middle Passage involved the deworlding of stolen persons and their recasting through the brand of blackness as all the same type of subordinate entity. As Yancy explains, "[t]he objective was to create a cultureless *thing*, an object that was defined within the same context as other commodities."[84] The process of creating blackness was thus the process of "stealing black people from themselves," in the words of Ta-Nehisi Coates.[85] Note how this process has distinct phenomenological implications for the branded and unbranded. For the unbranded, the process was one of learning to see the branded as ontologically demoted. For the branded, the process was one of being made to see oneself as ontologically demoted. In Yancy's words, "the African body, as early as the Middle Passage, was being marked and defined, disciplined to begin the process of seeing itself as thing-like, of undergoing the phenomenological process of returning to itself as that which is not free, but owned by another."[86] The project worked, and in time, as Jones explains, "Europeans would use the term *white* to describe themselves, no matter their nationality or, for that matter, their skin color; and *negro* or *black* would mean 'slave,' no matter the person's ethnicity."[87] Early Americans would eventually come to justify slavery "with theories of racial difference, theories that their colonial forbears had no incentive to create or invoke."[88] The distinctly American approach to "slavery evolved from a struggle for empire and a quest for mastery in the fields, and racial prejudice was more of an afterthought than a cause."[89]

The brand of blackness thus operated in two important dimensions. The brand designated the bearer as ontologically demoted in a general sense such that the branded person could be properly denied the full rights owed a person simpliciter. But the brand also specifically designated the bearer as one properly to be exploited; the brand of blackness operated as a permanent livery of sorts, allowing the world to identify the members of a servant class easily. The brand of race, a tool with the structure of in-order-to-designate-as-ontologically-subordinate, also transformed the bearers themselves into tools of a sort, beings with a structure of in-order-to-serve. By so doing, the person branded by race was stripped of their intrinsic value qua person and instead relegated to the instrumental value of a tool.[90] A person branded by race could thus be highly valued but only inasmuch as they played their role in service to the (white) world. By doing so, the branded person playing the role permitted them would become invisible, as tools do, receding into the background of the lives of the unbranded. And if the branded person instead opted to challenge the confines of servitude and assert their intrinsic value qua person, demanding a seat at the table as a person simpliciter, the branded person would become obtrusive as a tool out of place and court the punishing gaze of the (white) world. To crystallize and enforce the boundaries between the branded and the unbranded, American law devised a series of powerful and devastating innovations, the most important perhaps being the creation of a white right to harm Black persons and the concomitant loss of a Black right to self-defense.[91] This phenomenon defines and protects white privilege to the present day.[92]

The planter class of the 17th century American colonies lived under the threat of a coalition of the oppressed. In the early 17th century, there was significant overlap in the interests of lower-class and enslaved persons. While there is certainly evidence of segregationist ideologies in the early 17th century, there is ample evidence to suggest that the worlds of lower class and enslaved persons significantly intermingled.[93] The first slave ships arrived in the colonies in 1619, and by the 1660s, it had become clear to the planter class that there was a need to drive a legal and psychological wedge between laborers, but whiteness and blackness did not yet exist as such.[94] Enter, as McWhorter writes, "race as a tool for dividing a population into opposing factions."[95] In the words of Virginia's colonial governor William Gooch, this would be accomplished by affixing on enslaved persons "a perpetual Brand... by excluding them from that great Privilege of a Freeman."[96] Specifically, this was done "by lowering the legal status of free laborers of African descent and elevating that of free laborers of European descent."[97] As McWhorter explains, "[t]he 'brand' was not a punishment for crimes committed; it was a label and a status 'affixed' in order to neutralize and disempower, as well as to humiliate and degrade."[98] This was carried out through a system of laws "that marked them permanently as an underclass and distanced them physically and emotionally from other laborers who might otherwise share their interests."[99]

In the 1660s, we began to see the law distinguish between Black and white persons. Between 1660 and 1671, Virginia enacted laws permitting enslavement as punishment for crimes, but only for Black persons;[100] Virginia enacted laws punishing white persons assisting Black runaways;[101] Maryland and Virginia passed laws clarifying that while white persons could not serve lifelong servitude, Black persons would;[102] Maryland and Virginia clarified that conversion to Christianity did not mean emancipation;[103] Maryland declared white women who marry Black men a disgrace and bound their servitude to the lifetime of their husbands;[104] and Virginia, breaking from English law and adopting archaic Roman laws concerning livestock, decreed that a child's legal status would be determined by the mother, thereby turning enslaved women into slave factories and incentivizing master rape.[105]

Then, in 1676, a watershed moment came to pass in Bacon's Rebellion when a broad coalition of Virginians, including lower-class white persons as well as free and enslaved Black persons, took up arms against the colonial government.[106] As Kendi explains, wealthy planters learned from that experience that "poor Whites had to be forever separated from enslaved Blacks."[107] This led to a remarkable legal innovation: the codification of the white person's right to harm Black persons. After pardoning the white rebels involved in Bacon's Rebellion, Virginia passed a law imposing thirty lashes on "any negro or other slave" who "raises a hand . . . against any Christian," at a time when "Christian" meant white.[108] In 1705, the revised Virginia code confirmed that Black persons enjoyed no rights of self-defense, assembly, or suffrage; it stated that miscegenation resulted in "abominable mixtures"; it made slave patrols constituted by poor white persons compulsory; it ordered the sale of any property owned by enslaved persons so that the profit could be donated to the local parish (i.e., white) poor.[109] These codes were promulgated in churches so white persons, including and especially the uneducated, would know these new distinctions.[110]

A legal and psychological wedge had been driven in. By taking away the right of self-defense from Black persons, by creating a right to harm for white persons, the social bonds and shared interests between lower-class white and Black persons eroded. There was now a power asymmetry inherent in Black-white relations. How could they continue to socialize, romance, and organize if any difference of opinion carried with it the possibility of one of the parties being right per se and the other being whipped? As MacKinnon has noted, "[i]ntimate violation with impunity is an ultimate index of social power."[111] The possibility of a community incorporating white and Black persons was thus dealt a mortal blow because, as McWhorter explains, "[t]he social life that binds people together was no longer possible once the right to self-defense was rescinded."[112]

This power inequality would come to be internalized by lower-class white persons, it would endure through the centuries, and it would continue into the present such that Lyndon B. Johnson would eventually note that "[i]f you can convince the lowest white man he's better than the best colored man, he won't notice you're picking his pocket. Hell, give him somebody to look down on, and he'll empty his pockets for you."[113] As Kendi explains,

> [b]y the early eighteenth century, every Virginia county had a militia of landless Whites "ready in case of any sudden eruption of Indians or insurrection of Negroes." Poor Whites had risen into their lowly place in slave society—the armed defenders of planters—a place that would sow bitter animosity between them and enslaved Africans.[114]

In practice, this meant that these white militias worked against Black persons with impunity, reinforcing the understanding that as long as they were protecting white interests, they would be acquitted of any formal wrongdoing.

America emerged from this milieu, and the ontological brand of race allowed the mythical Founders to have their cake and eat it too.[115] When Thomas Jefferson refers to the "merciless Indian Savages" in the Declaration of Independence, or when the framers of our Constitution accept the enslavement of a fifth of the population, as Mills notes, "neither [they] nor [their] readers will experience any cognitive dissonance with earlier claims about the equality of all 'men,' since savages [and negroes] are not 'men' in the full sense of the word."[116] America's founding is thus the inauguration of a white world, one in which persons of color got to live, but only out of a white largesse that required them to know their place and stay in it; otherwise, the threat was always death.[117]

In 1791, the same year the Bill of Rights came into existence, the Haitian Revolution began and would become the first successful slave revolt the West had seen.[118] As Bacon's Rebellion had a century earlier, the Haitian Revolution struck fear in the hearts of slave owners, eliciting nightmares of Black mobs murdering white persons.[119] The Fugitive Slave Act was enacted two years later, creating a right and providing means to recover escaped slaves as well as punishing anyone who aided them.[120] The Fugitive Slave Act would be revamped in 1850, and by 1857, the white right to harm Black persons was so entrenched that the Supreme Court would come to explain in its *Dred Scott* decision that "neither the class of persons who had been imported as slaves nor their descendants, whether they had become free or not, were... intended to be included in the general words used in [the Declaration of Independence];" they "had for more than a century before been regarded as beings of an inferior order, and altogether unfit to associate with the white race, either in social or political relations; and so far inferior, that they had no rights which the white man was bound to respect; and that the negro might justly and lawfully be reduced to slavery for his benefit."[121] This fundamental distinction between whiteness and nonwhiteness, particularly between whiteness and blackness, was essential to the American project, and U.S. law was at its center. As Calvin Warren observes, "Antebellum politics circulates around the problem of Black being, the ontological terror that Black being is forced to bear in an antiblack world."[122]

Having successfully wielded the ontological power needed to brand non-Europeans as inherently inferior, the sky was the limit for a burgeoning white America. To the South, white America had access to a nearly limitless pool of slaves to feed its economic monster, and, to the West, white America recognized nothing but a manifest destiny and the savages and mongrels from which it needed to be wrested. At the same time, white Americans, the racially unbranded, the We of the We the People, could look out into that bright horizon and know that Providence had placed them there to be the exceptional light of the world.

Access to this world was restricted for other oppressed groups as well. The indentured servitude operating in the industrial North, for example, was hardly egalitarian. But the centrality of the brand of blackness infected even those dimensions; it was, in fact, essential to moving attention away from those axes of oppression. As Coates recounts, "'The two great divisions of society are not the rich and poor, but white and black,' said the great South Carolina senator John C. Calhoun. 'And all the former, the poor as well as the rich, belong to the upper class, and are respected and treated as equals.' And there it is—the right to break the black body as the meaning of their sacred equality."[123] Because whiteness meant not being excluded from the ranks of full personhood, whiteness was extremely valuable and operated as a type of property.[124] Like real property, the value of whiteness depended on defining and enforcing boundaries, and whiteness retained its ontological privilege only so long as the boundary between whiteness and nonwhiteness continued to be enforced, both formally through the law as well as informally through culture.[125]

The racial horrors of antebellum America are increasingly well documented. But it is important to underscore that no malice is needed on the part of the unbranded for ontological branding to happen or for its destructive effects to become endemic. We now understand that the simple fact of designating certain people as inferior—even in a completely fabricated manner and in a completely artificial environment—is powerful enough to create groups with real power inequalities from a set of otherwise undifferentiated persons. Thus, between 1620, when blackness and whiteness did not yet exist and enslaved persons were placed in a stratum more or less comparable to other oppressed groups, and 1857, when the Supreme Court of the United States stated that in America, Black persons had always been understood to be beings of an inferior order, as McWhorter notes, "[w]hat had once been a political scheme had become,... a kind of common sense."[126]

In America, the brand of blackness worked invisibly as a ubiquitous tool necessary for American life. Slave-owners, of course, did not see their slaves as enslaved persons whose enslavement was justified by a fabricated ontological demotion; instead, for them, slaves were simply inferior. Those in power experienced this distinction between person simpliciter and subordinate person as an ontic distinction: race was a mere fact that helped identify the type of entity in question. Blackness was simply a fact about being a Negro; whiteness was simply a fact about being a proper person. Blackness on a proper person or whiteness on a Negro was as nonsensical as redness on an orange or orangeness on an apple. This ontic distinction served as the basis to justify the fundamental distinction between slave-owner and slave: the white person and the Black person were different types of entities, where the fact of race was the distinguishing property.[127]

It is little wonder, then, that when slavery fell, the invisible brand remained. Despite a shift to understanding slavery as fundamentally incompatible with the American project, despite a newfound commitment to recognizing the "Negro" as U.S. citizen, the continuing understanding of race as fact evolved naturally into the Jim Crow regime. As Harold Cruse observed, "Emancipation elevated the Negro only to the position of semi-dependent man, not to that of an equal or independent being."[128] The antebellum Court in *Dred Scott* had articulated what turn-of-the-century America continued to understand and what the Court explained in *Plessy v. Ferguson*, that the purpose of the Reconstruction Amendments

> was undoubtedly to enforce the absolute equality of the two races before the law, but in the nature of things, it could not have been intended to abolish distinctions based upon color, or to enforce social, as distinguished from political, equality, or a commingling of the two races upon terms unsatisfactory to either.[129]

The ontic understanding of race underlying *Plessy* made the world fairly straightforward. You were either a Black citizen or a white citizen. Because there was no tiered citizenship, all citizens had equal access to rights granted to citizens. But the legal world was not like the natural world, and "citizenship" was not like "personhood." Thus, while in the legal world, all citizens were to be treated equally, these citizens came in kinds that were unequal by nature. Accordingly, legal equality would never, could never, and should never be taken to imply natural or social equality.[130]

In Redemption, the whitelash against Reconstruction, lynching became the marquee expression of the white right to harm Black persons. Though usually the supposed reaction to the rape of white women, lynching was at its root about putting "uppity" or "unruly" Black persons in their place, what McWhorter has called biopolitical terrorism.[131] On a larger scale, the same formulaic reaction to the alleged rape of white women led to incidents such as the 1921 Tulsa Race Massacre, in which 1,200 homes were destroyed and 300 mostly Black people were killed by a white mob working in complicity with white city government.[132] But the Tulsa Race Massacre was about nothing more and nothing less than quashing one of the most economically successful Black communities in America. As the Smithsonian Institution explains, "[t]he truth of the matter has to do with the threat that black power, black economic power, black cultural power, black success, posed to individuals and . . . the whole system of white supremacy. That's embedded within our nation's history."[133] Time and again, the dynamics underlying lynchings reveal a desperate need to police the boundaries of ontological brandedness, of who gets to participate freely in this (white) America and who is only supposed to play a supporting role.

MacKinnon's analysis of rape is illuminating in this regard. "Like lynching at one time, rape is socially permitted, though formally illegal," she explains, and "[t]hreat of sexual assault is threat of punishment *for being female*."[134] The racial dimension of oppression unfolds in a similar manner. Lynching was a formally illegal but socially permitted punishment *for being Black*—namely, for being a Black person who did not know their place. Of course, the victims of lynching were not only the persons lynched; lynching was a tool of terrorism that subjected all Black persons in the South to the constant threat of violence and death. This constant threat served as the backdrop for a (white) America that—North and South—purposefully excluded persons of color, especially Black persons, from socioeconomic opportunities and relegated them to roles in service of (white) America.[135] With every step, the brand of blackness was reinforced and highlighted the privilege of getting to be white, that is, the privilege of getting to be among the true heirs of the American project. This was particularly important for economically oppressed white persons for whom, as Yancy notes, "whiteness [was] a wage that paid handsomely in terms of public deference, psychological uplift, protection from harm, access to public parks, and better schools."[136]

In time, the Jim Crow world would fall before the declaration in *Brown v. Board* that separate is inherently unequal and the ushering in of the Civil Rights era. But, as Peller notes,

> The exercise of American racial power was not limited to the exclusion of Blacks from mainstream institutions. The construction of a discourse, an entire set of cultural practices, within which the open and explicit subordination of African Americans could seem normal was instead broadly inscribed into the everyday institutional culture of schools, offices, legislatures, streets, and neighborhoods, and possibly into the very meaning of what constitutes the rational and civilized.[137]

The Jim Crow regime had unfolded within a white supremacist world that was not magically changed by the legal requirement that Black persons be granted formal access to places where such access had been previously prohibited.[138] Nonetheless, U.S. law boldly proclaimed its new position that race did not matter because all men truly were created equal. And as if on cue—as told by (white) American mythology—Martin Luther King Jr. stepped onto the historical stage. Here was a specimen who exhibited the highest characteristics of humanity—he was educated, reasonable, moral, Christian, and nonviolent—the same characteristics that scientific racism once concluded were impossible for the lesser races.[139] Through *Brown*, the Civil Rights Act, and the eventual canonization of Martin Luther King in the popular psyche, (white) America came to believe that it had reneged on *Plessy*'s ontological conclusion that blackness and whiteness evinced membership in groups that were unequal by nature, while at the same time protecting the racial inequalities *Plessy* had created and maintained.

NOTHING TO SEE HERE: TURNING A BLIND EYE TO RACE

Race is not a fact about us as mere things; race is a tool used to manufacture white privilege by subordinating those branded as nonwhite. The brand of race works by ascribing ontological meaning to otherwise meaningless facts. Whiteness was created by branding all non-Europeans as subordinate entities and privileging Europeans as persons simpliciter. In the United States, persons of African descent were branded with blackness, where blackness designated someone an in-order-to-serve the interests of the white world. Race is inherently a power dynamic between privileged white persons and subordinated persons of color.

But U.S. law has from the beginning concealed the tool nature of race by treating race as a simple fact about us as mere things. The changes that have transpired in U.S. law vis-à-vis race correspond to shifting views only on whether the assumed fact of racial difference corresponds to any meaningful ontological differences between the races. U.S. law has moved from an explicitly white supremacist social ontology that placed great significance on the fact of race because racial groups were understood as unequal by nature to what is now a formally colorblind social ontology according to which race is meaningless because all individuals are defined as equivalent before the law. But by consistently maintaining the false ontology of race-as-fact and concealing the tool nature of race, U.S. law has pursued greater and greater formal equality while leaving intact the underlying structures that maintain a (white) America that privileges whiteness and subordinates persons of color, especially Black persons.

Antebellum U.S. law espoused a white supremacist social ontology according to which the fact of race was important because different races were understood to have different ontologies. White people and Negroes were different kinds of things: white people were superior; Negroes were inferior. But this social ontology was predicated on a lie. Race was never simply a fact; race was a tool, and it was only through the intervention of law that the lie of race-as-fact became scientific truth and common sense. U.S. law made (white) America a world by and for white persons within which nonwhite persons were permitted to exist only to the degree that they stayed in their allotted spaces and served their designated functions. The nonwhite person who challenged their space or role always faced the possibility of violence or death.

U.S. law's espousal of a white supremacist social ontology was temporarily challenged after the Civil War. The Reconstruction Amendments sought to erase the brand of servitude imposed on Black persons. But even then, there was no challenge to the false ontology of race-as-fact. Race was understood to be a fact about us, and races were understood to correspond to natural kinds; the challenge was only to the significance of this fact, viz., whether Black people were inferior to white people. This challenge was short-lived, however. The constitutional safeguards of liberty and equality provided by the Reconstruction Amendments were reduced to formalities that safeguarded white privilege and Black subordination as U.S. law entered the Jim Crow era. U.S. law then confirmed the same white supremacist social ontology espoused in antebellum law, where whiteness and blackness were understood to be simple facts that corresponded to races that were unequal by nature. In fact, the races were so unequal, as the Supreme Court itself clarified, that law could do nothing to bridge the ontological distance between them. Even with the Reconstruction Amendments in place, U.S. law thus continued to safeguard white supremacy by permitting the devaluation and exploitation of persons of color, especially Black persons, and subjecting them to the constant threat of violence and death.

In the Civil Rights era, U.S. law's espousal of a white supremacist social ontology was again temporarily challenged.[140] The underlying false ontology remained intact, however, and race continued to be understood as a fact about us; the challenge was only to the significance of the fact of race. During the Civil Rights era, U.S. law rejected its expressly white supremacist social ontology and replaced it with one in which all individuals were equal by definition. This meant that while race remained a fact about us, it was now deemed a meaningless fact in the eyes of the law. The U.S. law of our current colorblind era safeguards white supremacy through ontological legerdemain. By proclaiming the equality of all before it, the law appears to reject its commitment to white supremacy, but the only thing it does is define away the problem of an ontological inequality that law itself has steadily built and safeguarded over the past 400 years. By declaring race an insignificant fact, U.S. law effectively prevents any action that can meaningfully counteract white supremacy. The reality is that U.S. law continues its protection of a (white) America in which persons of color, especially Black persons, are devalued, exploited, and subject to an ever-present threat of violence and death.

Colorblindness as racial justice has an intuitive appeal for many because it resonates with the elegant Aristotelian principle that justice is treating likes alike and injustice is treating likes unalike. This principle has animated much of the Western understanding of justice and served as the foundation for the liberal commitment to the protection of universal human equality. If it is the case that all persons are equal, and if it is the case, that our government's *raison d'etre* is to safeguard our rights to life, liberty, and the pursuit of happiness, any attempt to introduce distinctions between persons becomes automatically suspect. If I have a bag full of identical marbles, it would be nonsensical to sort them by type; if I have a bag full of marbles to be treated as identical, the mandate is violated by distinguishing between them. Accordingly, if it is the case that race is meaningless because it does nothing to alter the fundamental human equality enjoyed by all persons, distinguishing between persons by race becomes unjust per se.[141]

This view, what Manne might call the "naïve view,"[142] or what Kendi calls the "folktale of racism,"[143] is the one espoused by U.S. law today. Under this view, because everyone is equal, racial justice means treating everyone equally regardless of their race, and racial injustice means treating people differently on the basis of their race; a racist is someone who treats people differently on the basis of their race, and a non-racist is someone who does not. Under this view, racial injustice occurs through immoral choices or epistemic errors. Distinguishing between racial groups might come out of conscious racism of a deliberate rejection of the idea that racial groups are ontologically equal, and this rejection would fall under the category of immoral choice. But distinguishing between racial groups could also come about in a non-deliberate manner. Racism could result from epistemic error, a misunderstanding of alikes as unalike, whether because of cultural upbringing, cognitive biases, or both.

Under the naïve view, racism entails distinguishing between ontologically equal entities, that is, treating likes unalike, racial injustice is power-neutral, and equidirectional. White people are as capable of being racist against Black people as Black people are of being racist against white people, and we must be ever vigilant of treating likes unalike.[144] Accordingly, the legalized racial injustices the United States saw in slavery and then under the Jim Crow era were the result of a critical mass of racists being able to enact racially unjust laws within a democratic system. But things changed once a critical mass of non-racists stood up against that codified injustice. With increasing breadth, the law changed to better protect the individual from racial injustice. Beginning with the Reconstruction Amendments and continuing through the Civil Rights era, separate came to be understood as inherently unequal because individuals are inherently equal. Today, the legal standard is colorblindness because we have finally arrived where the law should have been all along: affirming that everyone should be treated the same regardless of race.

But this view is predicated on ontological sleight of hand, and three contemporary Supreme Court decisions are particularly helpful in bringing it to light. In *Adarand v. Peña* (1995),[145] the Court confirmed its understanding that race is a meaningless fact, that all individuals are by definition ontological equals, and that racial justice is, therefore, colorblindness. Accordingly, governmental programs that grant preferential treatment to people of color are almost always invalid. A decade later, in *Parents Involved in Community Schools v. Seattle School District No. 1* (2007),[146] the Court clarified that U.S. law could intervene to remedy specific harms to specific individuals caused by specific governmental failures to be colorblind, but U.S. law could otherwise do nothing to interfere with social disparities between racial groups because these were merely the result of private choices made by equal individuals that U.S. law was bound to respect. Nonetheless, the *Parents Involved* decision acknowledged that, in certain contexts, racial diversity could be a permissible goal under U.S. law. But in *Schuette v. Coalition to Defend Affirmative Action* (2014),[147] the Court clarified that while racial diversity can be permissible, it is not required; what is required, however, is respect for individual choice, and if a white majority of individuals choose to take diversity off the table entirely, U.S. law will protect that choice in the name of colorblindness.

In *Adarand v Peña*, the United States Department of Transportation had awarded a prime contract to Mountain Gravel Construction Company. Under the contract, Mountain Gravel would receive additional compensation if it awarded subcontracts to businesses certified as Disadvantaged Business Enterprises (DBEs). A DBE was defined as a small business controlled by socially and economically disadvantaged individuals.[148] Importantly, per the act, persons of color and women were presumptively socially and economically disadvantaged.[149] The Gonzales Construction Company and Adarand Constructors, Inc. submitted competing bids for one of the Mountain Gravel subcontracts. Gonzales was certified as a DBE (the decision does not reveal how Gonzales obtained the certification), Adarand was not, and Gonzales won the subcontract, even though Adarand's bid was the lowest.[150]

Adarand filed suit in U.S. District Court, claiming that the presumption that persons of color were socially and economically disadvantaged individuals was discriminatory on the basis of race in violation of the Federal Government's Fifth Amendment obligation not to deny anyone equal protection of the laws.[151] The District Court sided with the government, upholding the DBE program's presumptions of social and economic disadvantage on the basis of race. For its part, the Court of Appeals affirmed because it found the DBE regulations to be "narrowly tailored to achieve [their] significant governmental purpose of providing subcontracting opportunities for small disadvantaged business enterprises."[152]

The Supreme Court disagreed. In her opinion for the Court, Justice Sandra Day O'Connor explained that while the Court of Appeals had properly analyzed the case under a standard established by the Supreme Court itself in a prior decision, that old standard would be overruled and replaced with one far stricter. To justify, O'Connor explained that "racial discriminations are in most circumstances irrelevant and therefore prohibited" because "[d]istinctions between citizens solely because of their ancestry are by their very nature odious to a free people whose institutions are founded upon the doctrine of equality."[153] Accordingly, "whenever the government treats any person unequally because of his or her race, that person has suffered an injury that falls squarely within the language and spirit of the Constitution's guarantee of equal protection."[154] Importantly, this harm is always caused by specific action and always suffered by individuals: "it is the individual who is entitled to judicial protection against classifications based upon his racial or ethnic background because such distinctions impinge upon personal rights," viz., the right to be treated as equal to every other citizen.[155] The upshot of the *Adarand* decision is that "the government may treat people differently because of their race only for the most compelling reasons. Accordingly, we hold today that all racial classifications, imposed by whatever federal, state, or local governmental actor, must be analyzed by a reviewing court under strict scrutiny."[156]

Adarand helps disclose the social ontology underlying current U.S. law. Race is a fact about us—a hereditary fact—and an irrelevant one; because all individuals are equally (un)raced before the law, justice requires that laws be colorblind with a view to moving society toward a point when race will no longer matter. Because U.S. law defines all persons as equal vis-à-vis race, and because justice is treating likes alike, law causes harm when it distinguishes between persons on the basis of race. When I sort my bag of identical marbles by provenance, a sorted marble can complain that I'm treating it unequally to every other marble—the very act of sorting harms each of the sorted marbles—but we would not say that I have harmed the groups, after all, the groups should not even exist and to the degree that they do, it is because of the impermissible sorting. Because racial distinctions are meaningless, all individuals are equivalent qua raced, and racial groups do not exist, hence "the basic principle that the Fifth and Fourteenth Amendments to the Constitution protect persons, not groups."[157] By the same token, discriminatory action will not be evaluated in terms of harm done to racial groups; after all, racial groups, do not exist before the eyes of the law.

Beyond understanding that all races are equal, this reasoning suggests that we have a fundamental right to be raceless, that I have a right to have no race because recognizing race puts me in a category, and I have a right to not be categorized. Some people may happen to be Black or happen to be white, but there is only one objective reality, the one in which all are equal and equally raceless before the law, the one on which America is founded. But this position ignores that in (white) America, racelessness is whiteness, and Blackness exists within and against white occupation. This reduction of race to the ontic, made even by some liberal white persons, has served, as Peller notes, as "an indirect defense of status quo social and institutional practices" by failing to understand the "cultural manifestations of racial power" that operate ontologically, resulting in persons with distinct and unequal access to distinct and unequal worlds.[158]

In his concurring opinion in *Adarand*, Justice Antonin Scalia was more direct than the majority opinion: "[i]n the eyes of the government, we are just one race here. It is American."[159] According to Scalia, this stems from the "Constitution's focus upon the individual, . . . and its rejection of dispositions based on race."[160] Thus, while "[i]individuals who have been wronged by unlawful racial discrimination should be made whole," the Constitution does not recognize racial groups, and "under our Constitution there can be no such thing as either a creditor or debtor race."[161] In other words, an individual may well have been harmed by governmental discrimination on the basis of race (as in this case, Adarand was understood to be), and the government may owe that individual some remedial action, but it would be nonsensical under this view to say that Black persons, or blackness, or the Black world has been harmed or that white persons, or whiteness, or (white) America bear any responsibility. Per the Scalia view, if U.S. law were to address racial disparities by affirmatively attempting to increase participation of persons of color in historically white spaces, we would be engaging in "racial entitlement" and thereby "reinforce and preserve for future mischief the way of thinking that produced slavery, race privilege and race hatred."[162] Accordingly, "government can never have a 'compelling interest' in discriminating on the basis of race in order to 'make up' for past racial discrimination in the opposite direction."[163]

Per the Scalia view, the problem with slavery and Jim Crow is that U.S. law allowed "racial entitlement" for white persons. This was wrong, and it was wrong because racial entitlement presumes that races are real things, but the Constitution does not recognize races, only individuals, and for the law to see an individual as raced is to violate that individual. Thus, the remedy can never be to provide racial entitlements—even with the intention to address past harms—because the very recognition of race constitutes evil, and two wrongs don't make a right. To provide preferential treatment to some necessarily implies harm to others. It is a zero-sum game, just like slavery and apartheid, and the only solution can be colorblindness. Under this view, then, racial injustice is power neutral and equidirectional: anybody from any racial group can perpetrate racial injustice on anybody from any other racial group.

Justice Clarence Thomas, in his concurring opinion, underscores this power-neutral understanding of racial injustice: "there is a 'moral [and] constitutional equivalence' between laws designed to subjugate a race and those that distribute benefits on the basis of race in order to foster some current notion of equality."[164] Because "[racial] classifications ultimately have a destructive impact on the individual and our society . . ., under our Constitution, the government may not make distinctions on the basis of race."[165] But Thomas adds a disturbing ontological maneuver to his criticism of the DBE program at issue in *Adarand*: "These programs stamp minorities with a badge of inferiority and may cause them to develop dependencies or to adopt an attitude that they are 'entitled' to preferences."[166] In other words, according to Thomas, governmental programs that expressly seek to facilitate the participation of persons of color in historically white spaces both mark persons of color as presumptively unqualified (before the white gaze) and can result in persons of color whose being in the world is dependent or entitled, that is, parasitic, instead of a being in the world becoming of an individual among equals.

All of these concerns point to one means—colorblindness—for the sake of one end—postracialism. O'Connor argued that racial classifications by the government ought to be subject to strict scrutiny, even in the case of classifications intended to help historically oppressed groups, because such preferences "can only exacerbate rather than reduce racial prejudice, [and] it will delay the time when race will become a truly irrelevant, or at least insignificant, factor."[167] Scalia and Thomas express an even clearer liberal colorblindness focused on the individual's right to be free from racial classification and a view of racial justice as a time when race will no longer be an issue. But these very views—that race is an insignificant fact about us and that racial justice is a world where race no longer matters—are also expressed in the dissenting opinions. Justice David Souter, for example, explains that while it "may be that some members of the historically favored race are hurt by" affirmative action programs, "this price is considered reasonable . . . in part because it is a price to be paid only temporarily; . . . the assumption is that the effects will themselves recede into the past, becoming attenuated and finally disappearing."[168] And in her dissenting opinion, Justice Ruth Bader Ginsburg expressed an understanding that the DBE program at issue entailed a permissible racial classification in part because it was ontologically remedial, viz., one "made to hasten the day when 'we are just one race.'"[169]

Such liberal colorblindness with an eye toward postracialism is predicated on an understanding of the individual that rejects any type of an embodied personhood always already in a world. Under this view, the individual is a monad with a fundamental right to not be ascribed membership in any group because, in the eyes of the law, the individual is indistinguishable from any other individual. The false ontology that undergirds this naïve notion of equality attempts to conceal the significant disparities that exist between whiteness and nonwhiteness in (white) America, disparities that were created and are maintained by U.S. law. More broadly, for the unbranded—for example, hetero, cis, white, able, affluent males—a legal system that sees them as identical units may well make sense and foster an egalitarian meritocracy. But the ontologically branded, that is, the vast majority of humanity, are always already in a world that has demoted them, and their membership in their brand group is as real as it is involuntary.[170] To argue that law should be blind to this in the name of individual liberty is to attempt to define away the reality of group oppression. The powerful formula of liberalism plus the ontological brand of race has yielded one inevitable result—a white supremacist state that sees itself as egalitarian. This approach conceals the ontological dimension of race. Approaching race as a mere fact puts the focus on racial equality and removes from the conversation any question of power inequalities inherent in race itself because individuals have been defined as equal and races have been defined away. It is this approach that Kendi has called "the most racist idea to date," namely, that since discrimination has been eliminated and we are now operating under a meritocracy, "since Blacks were still losing the race, the racial disparities and their continued losses must be their fault."[171]

In *Parents Involved in Community Schools v. Seattle School District No. 1*, the Supreme Court considered whether the Seattle, Washington and Jefferson County, Kentucky public school districts were constitutionally permitted to use race as a factor in determining student school placement for the sake of promoting racial integration within the schools. The Seattle School District allowed students to apply to any high school in the District. Since certain schools often became oversubscribed when too many students chose them as their first choice, the District used a system of tiebreakers to decide which students would be admitted to the oversubscribed schools. The first tiebreaker rule involved favoring applicants who already had siblings in the school at issue. The second tiebreaker rule used the applicants' race (defined as either "white" or "nonwhite") to ensure that the student body at the school at issue reflected the proportion of white to nonwhite students in the district at large within ten percentage points.[172] For its part, Jefferson County required that Black students constitute no fewer than 15 percent, and no more than 50 percent, of the student body of the schools at issue.[173]

The Seattle and Jefferson County school integration plans were each challenged in court, and each plan was affirmed as proper by their respective District and Circuit Courts, but the Supreme Court disagreed.[174] Writing for the Court, Chief Justice John Roberts concluded that the measures at issue violated the Equal Protection Clause of the Fourteenth Amendment. "Racial integration or diversity," as Roberts described it, was not a compelling state interest, and the measures at issue thus failed to pass strict scrutiny.[175] U.S. law would be permitted to adopt race-conscious measures in the realm of public education for the sake of integration only if and as necessary to remedy past de jure segregation.[176] In other words, U.S. law was permitted to see race only to the degree that it was necessary to return to a baseline state of law that does not see race at all.

The predicate in all this is a violation of U.S. law on the proscription on seeing race. Roberts' reasoning relies on a fundamental distinction between governmental and individual acts. To the degree that the law itself caused injury by seeing and acting on the basis of an individual's race, it is permitted to enact race-conscious measures to undo this harm. In public education, for example, impermissible segregation is defined as de jure segregation, that is, "legally separate schools for students of different races."[177] Such segregation is unconstitutional because it entails U.S. law treating individuals differently on the basis of race. But the law is not permitted to enact race-conscious measures to remedy segregation caused by individual or societal discrimination, which was, according to Roberts, the situation that Seattle and Jefferson County faced.

As Richard Rothstein recounts,

> The chief justice noted that racially homogenous housing arrangements in these cities had led to racially homogenous student bodies in neighborhood schools. He observed that racially separate neighborhoods might result from "societal discrimination" but said that remedying discrimination "not traceable to [government's] own actions" can never justify a constitutionally acceptable, racially conscious, remedy. "The distinction between segregation by state action and racial imbalance caused by other factors has been central to our jurisprudence .... Where [racial imbalance] is a product not of state action but of private choices, it does not have constitutional implications." Because neighborhoods in Louisville and Seattle had been segregated by private choices, he concluded, school districts should be prohibited from taking purposeful action to reverse their own resulting segregation.[178]

In Roberts' words, "[a]ccepting racial integration or diversity as a compelling state interest would justify the imposition of racial proportionality throughout American society, contrary to our repeated recognition that '[a]t the heart of the Constitution's guarantee of equal protection lies the simple command that the Government must treat citizens as individuals, not as simply components of a racial, religious, sexual or national class.'"[179] Ultimately, Roberts proclaimed, the problem and the solution are really not that complicated because "[t]he way to stop discrimination on the basis of race is to stop discriminating on the basis of race." [180]

Note the assumption underlying this view: race is an insignificant fact about us as mere things.[181] Under this approach, race is something like our height or blood type, which may be relevant in certain contexts but can never really serve as a legitimate basis for treating persons differently. But the colorblindness of today's U.S. law is Jim Crow in a wig.[182] The national shame that is *Plessy* lives on in *Parents Involved*.[183] *Plessy* was about policing racial hierarchies and boundaries, about making clear that whatever legal equality meant, it did not mean ontological equality. The social ontology implied in *Plessy* was one according to which race was a fact corresponding to ontological distinctions: white persons and Black persons were by nature different kinds of things, and blackness was inferior to whiteness. Whereas the law could guarantee equality qua citizenship before the law, the law could never erase the ontological inequality that inhered in race by nature. The result was that U.S. law could make Black and white persons legal equals, but U.S. law could never make them social equals.

Parents Involved purports to be diametrically opposed to *Plessy*. *Parents Involved* purports to take precisely this history of racism into account in its demand that the law be blind to a person's race. But the colorblindness of *Parents Involved* is a Trojan horse for *Plessy*'s ontology. Under *Parents Involved*, race remains a fact about us, but it is now an insignificant fact given that white and nonwhite persons are by definition equal before the law. Race thus does not matter, and the law does wrong to recognize racial distinctions because the law's utmost mandate is to respect the individual as such and treat individual choices as sacrosanct. Accordingly, to the degree that certain communities are majority white and affluent, unless it can be proven that these are the result of intentional discrimination by U.S. law itself, these communities must be understood to be as they are because of the private choices made by the individuals that comprise these communities. By the same token, to the degree that there are communities that happen to be majority Black and economically disadvantaged, absent proof of deliberate segregation by U.S. law, these must be understood to exist by virtue of the private choices of the individuals in those communities.[184] Importantly, according to *Parents Involved*, we cannot lift the hood of individuals' private choices for the sake of some nebulous interest in diversity. In other words, the distinctions that exist between the majority Black and majority white communities, whatever these may be, are the result of private choices, and law has no business interfering with those sacrosanct private distinctions.[185]

Under *Plessy*'s ontology, the social inequalities experienced by Black and white persons corresponded to differences in nature that the law could not address. But these differences were created and maintained by U.S. law. Under *Parents Involved*, the social inequalities experienced by Black and white persons correspond to differences in private choices that the law cannot address. But, again, these differences were themselves products of U.S. law; what counts as nature or private choice is determined by exertions of public power.[186] Similarly, in the same way, *Plessy* asserted that any stigma associated with blackness was self-imposed, thereby blaming Black persons for their subordination, *Parents Involved* implies that segregation in the present day is the problem of the communities that choose to remain segregated.[187] It is, after all, a free country. No one is telling these families not to move into historically white spaces. They must be choosing not to do so. In *Plessy* and *Parents Involved*, the end result is the same: a (white) America in which the law cannot interfere with the very social inequalities between white and Black communities that the law itself created and maintains.[188]

Nonetheless, while U.S. law may not seek racial diversity as a general goal, it may, as *Parents Involved* explained, permissibly consider race for the sake of curating a diverse student body within public higher education.[189] In this specific context, U.S. law is permitted to see race, but only as one factor among many for the sake of a broadly diverse student body. In other words, U.S. law is allowed in this limited space to distinguish between individuals when race would be only one factor among many to consider. The State would run afoul of its obligations, however, if it were to reduce an individual to membership in a racial group by adopting something like a quota. The state can see race while seeing the individual qua individual; the state cannot see race when seeing an individual qua member of a racial group.

In *Schuette v. Coalition to Defend Affirmative Action*, however, the Supreme Court clarified that U.S. law would not protect even that very modest interest in racial diversity if it conflicted with the interests of the white majority. *Schuette* is part of a series of decisions concerning Michigan's attempts to increase racial diversity in its public higher education institutions. While the U.S. Supreme Court invalidated some measures as impermissible governmental discrimination on the basis of race, the Court nonetheless allowed that race could be one among many factors considered in admissions for the sake of diversity, given that diversity benefits all students. But even this watered-down commitment to racial diversity was too much for voters in Michigan (a majority of whom are white), and in 2006 a Michigan proposition to amend the state constitution passed to prohibit the government from "discriminat[ing] against, or grant[ing] preferential treatment to, any individual or group on the basis of race, sex, color, ethnicity, or national origin in the operation of public employment, public education, or public contracting."[190]

With jurisprudence like *Parents Involved* as the background, it was clear that the amendment would mean prohibiting diversity efforts in the name of colorblindness. The amendment was accordingly challenged in the courts as an unconstitutional violation of the Equal Protection Clause. The challenge reached the Supreme Court, and the Court sided with the Michigan white majority. In his plurality opinion, Justice Anthony Kennedy explained that "[t]he question here concerns not the permissibility of race-conscious admissions policies under the Constitution but whether, and in what manner, voters in the States may choose to prohibit the consideration of racial preferences in governmental decisions, in particular with respect to school admissions."[191] In other words, the issue was not whether U.S. law permitted racial diversity as a (limited) goal in higher education, which it did; the issue was whether U.S. law could prohibit a majority of individuals from choosing to ban racial diversity as a goal altogether. The Court held that it could not. U.S. law again subordinated the interests of persons of color by privileging the white majority's right to control its white world.

Of note, the Court's decision equates "preferential treatment" with "discrimination."[192] Under this view, any time U.S. law confers any discernible benefit whatsoever to a particular racial group or people of color generally, it is a per se act of racial discrimination. In the extremely narrow context of increasing general diversity in public higher education, this discrimination is considered permissible because diversity is considered a general good. In other words, if in the name of a more diverse student body, certain white students are excluded that would not have been excluded if racial diversity had not been a goal, that discrimination against those white students is tolerable given the permissible interest in diversity which itself also benefits the white students that are included. But diversity is not required by the Constitution. What is required is respect for private choices among individuals. In Michigan, that meant that voters were permitted to set aside interests in diversity, that is, voters were permitted to set aside interests in increasing the inclusion of persons of color in historically white spaces in the name of colorblindness. In other words, *Schuette* confirms that U.S. law will protect a white majority's right to maintain white control over (white) America, all in the name of colorblind racial justice.[193] As Jack Balkin and Reva Siegel aptly describe it, "[i]n today's world, the language of constitutional equality has been hijacked and co-opted to protect those with privilege from the claims of those who lack it."[194]

It is not an accident that some of the most foundational jurisprudence concerning race is about educational institutions. After all, one of the tried and true ways we have to address socioeconomic injustices is by creating greater access to quality education.[195] But to do so would threaten the ontological inequalities that uphold (white) America. It is no surprise, then, that U.S. law has sided with protecting segregation, nor is it a surprise that U.S. law has sided with protecting the power of the police to shoot first and justify later,[196] or sided with the ability of white communities to locate toxic waste facilities in communities of color,[197] or sided with a criminal justice system that acknowledges racial injustices but accepts them as permissible.[198] In all these examples, and in countless more, the common thread is the same: U.S. law protects the right to harm persons of color for the sake of safeguarding (white) America.

Despite significant changes in the import of race throughout the history of U.S. law, our legal understanding of race has operated consistently within the ontic dimension, always assuming that the term *race* refers to a constellation of biological properties that help categorize the type of thing we are. But because there is an ontological dimension to race, because race is not a fact but a tool, continuing this ontic march toward racial equality, no matter how many advances we make, will continue to fail to address the power inequalities inherent in race, thereby allowing our legal system to continue safeguarding the interests of white supremacy. Today we live in an era where de jure racial discrimination is impermissible and our laws are largely colorblind. And yet this colorblind legal system has still produced a society where we routinely engage in the presumptive criminalization and mass incarceration of an entire sector of society, where the testimony of Black witnesses is regularly devalued, and where Black persons are even believed to feel less pain than white persons.[199] In 2022, in the United States, over forty million persons are still branded with blackness, and their treatment as ontologically demoted continues to go largely unaddressed because, in (white) America, Black lives simply do not matter as much as white ones.

The white privilege U.S. law safeguards is at its core an ontological supremacy predicated on the subordination of persons of color.[200] This was true in colonial America, it was true in antebellum America, it was true in Jim Crow America, and it remains true today. The horrifying spectacle of lynching, after all, faded only once institutional alternatives to manage unruliness came online.[201] Fast forward to the present, and the routine extrajudicial killing of Black persons with the *nihil obstat* of U.S. law is revealed to be an unbroken continuation of (white) America's right to beat, rape, rob, and pillage the Black body.[202] The Black person killed extrajudicially, in Coates' words, is "not killed by a single officer so much as he was murdered by his country and all the fears that have marked [his body] from birth."[203]

Consider George Floyd. Here was a man murdered by a police officer who knelt on his neck for nine minutes.[204] Much of America cheered when the murderer was convicted. But a quarter of America did not.[205] And the conviction, in the face of countless and ongoing extrajudicial killings of Black persons at the hands of police that go unpunished, only serves as a chilling illustration of the lengths to which law enforcement has to go to be considered excessive. U.S. law largely immunizes police officers from prosecution in extrajudicial killings through qualified immunity, an invention of the Supreme Court.[206]

Consider also Trayvon Martin. Here was a teenager walking through a neighborhood. He is confronted by a man who pursued Martin because, according to him, Martin looked "suspicious."[207] Martin looked like he did not belong. Martin's brand of Black maleness preceded him. What to do? Martin could have perhaps accepted that he had become obtrusive as an out-of-place tool.[208] Martin could perhaps have smiled broadly and kindly, apologized for being where he was not supposed to be, turned around, and left the way he came. Martin could have, in other words, understood that he was being confronted by the gaze of a (white) America demanding that he know and stay in his place. We cannot know for certain, but it seems Martin did not. Instead, it seems that Martin asserted his right to simply be there, that is, to be as any person simpliciter would expect to be. But Martin was not a person simpliciter; Martin was a subordinate person branded with blackness, and he was killed for challenging that color line. For his part, Martin's killer was acquitted on the grounds that he was defending himself. And he was, in a way: he and the legal system that acquitted him were defending themselves against challenges to the boundary between brandedness and unbrandedness.

Seeing Black persons killed with legal impunity creates in the Black viewer a "potent and confusing sense of embodied powerlessness, emptiness, stress, fear, nausea."[209] The result is a Foucauldian panopticon within which Black persons experience themselves always seen and at all times, "worry[ing] about their every action in front of White people, just as their enslaved brethren worried about their every action in front of their enslavers,"[210] This creates a pressure for "[s]elf-surveillance or getting the black body to regulate itself in the physical absence of the white gaze."[211]

But unaddressed murders are only the most extreme and visible instantiations of the everyday white right to harm Black persons, a phenomenon woven into all dimensions of present-day (white) America. Consider Coates' own experience, as written to his son:

> You were almost five years old. The theater was crowded, and when we came out we rode a set of escalators down to the ground floor. As we came off, you were moving at the dawdling speed of a small child. A white woman pushed you and said, "Come on!" Many things now happened at once. There was the reaction of any parent when a stranger lays a hand on the body of his or her child. And there was my own insecurity in my ability to protect your black body. . . . I was only aware that someone had invoked their right over the body of my son. I turned and spoke to this woman, and my words were hot with all of the moment and all of my history. She shrunk back, shocked. A white man standing nearby spoke up in her defense. I experienced this as his attempt to rescue the damsel from the beast. He had made no such attempt on behalf of my son. And he was now supported by other white people in the assembling crowd. The man

came closer. He grew louder. I pushed him away. He said, "I could have you arrested!" ... Which is to say: "I could take your body."[212]

The Jim Crow era is behind us, we live in an age of presumed racial equality, and yet, somehow, a white adult enjoys the right to shove a Black child without consequence, and the child's Black parent has no right to defend the child or himself. In this exchange, the white woman is primordially innocent/correct, and Coates is primordially guilty/incorrect. As Yancy writes, "her perspective, her subjectivity, is deemed the only important perspective, the one that makes a difference, the one that has historically reaped the benefit of recognition within the context of white North America."[213]

U.S. criminal law operates under the foundational principle that all persons are presumed innocent until proven guilty. But in this arena, we again see the disparity between brandedness and unbrandedness. While this principle can be generally relied upon by the unbranded, the branded are not afforded the same access to the same justice.[214] In contemporary America, white persons are primordially innocent, but Black persons are primordially guilty.[215] As Yancy puts it, "the Black body is condemned before it even acts; it has always already committed a crime;"[216] "from the perspective of whiteness, the Black body is criminality itself."[217] This state of primordial guilt is a result of the ontological subordination Black persons have been made to suffer. White is pure while Black is defiled; white is good while Black is bad; white is beautiful while Black is ugly; white is innocent while Black is guilty.[218] Our legal system purports to guarantee the principle of presumptive innocence, that, as Naomi Zack explains, "those who are innocent will be left alone by the government, as represented by the police, and those who are guilty, such as the police in killing wrongfully, will be punished."[219] For the unbranded, this is taken for granted. It is assumed that their lives unfold under the protection of this guarantee. But for the branded, particularly for Black persons, these would-be guarantees are "aspirations" at best.[220]

Because the brand of race is pervasive and invisible, it confuses types of knowing. By always already being in a world that demotes persons of color and renders blackness primordially guilty, we preconsciously *know* that a Black person is guilty of a crime. This deep knowledge acquired through the mastery of the tools of our world is what Yancy calls "epistemic violence."[221] Consider how naturally this all plays out. When George Zimmerman was on trial for killing Trayvon Martin, he claimed that he had acted in self-defense. At the end of the trial, the court gave the following instructions to the jury:

> In deciding whether George Zimmerman was justified in the use of deadly force, you must judge him by the circumstances by which he was surrounded at the time the force was used. The danger facing George Zimmerman need not have been actual; however, to justify the use of deadly force, the appearance of

danger must have been so real that a reasonably cautious and prudent person under the same circumstances would have believed that the danger could be avoided only through the use of that force. Based upon appearances, George Zimmerman must have actually believed that the danger was real.[222]

The danger need not have been real. Zimmerman need only have believed the danger was real. And if a reasonable person would have believed under those circumstances that deadly force was the only way to avoid that believed danger, Zimmerman was justified in killing Martin. But what is reasonable? And to whom? If within (white) America, Black is presumptively dangerous and guilty, might not one always already be reasonably and profoundly afraid of Black persons?

Reflecting on the killing of Michael Brown, Yancy notes that in the imagination of many at the time, Brown "wasn't unarmed. He was armed with his incredibly strong, scary self." "In other words," Yancy explains, "Brown's body was racially transmogrified, perceived as terrifying, bloodcurdling. His body was weaponized as it is perceived as incredibly strong, 'scary,' and dare I say—Black."[223] Ultimately, Yancy explains,

> my Black body, one that is fungible vis-à-vis other Black bodies that are deemed criminal, scary, monstrous, demonic, has already undergone a process of racial interpellation that has done metaphysical violence, where, historically, the governing norms of white philosophical anthropology marked Black bodies as disgusting and occluded from the realm of the conceptually white anthropos . . . . [M]y Black body . . . is part of a larger social integument—a social skin—that has claimed my body to be ontologically problematic.[224]

"Black being," Warren notes, "is always already under attack; peace, within an antiblack world, is a fallacy (much like freedom). The metaphysical infrastructure that supports the fiction of the white human is sustained by antiblack violence."[225]

This is the triumph of the invisibility of white supremacy. In (white) America, one, that is, the collective *one* that Heidegger describes as the invisible background structure of shared social relations, is a person simpliciter.[226] In (white) America, one is white.[227] Because whiteness is predicated on the subordination of nonwhiteness, and because the subordination of nonwhiteness is predicated on persons of color staying in their place, in (white) America, one is afraid of persons of color, especially Black persons, who seem not to know their place.[228] Borrowing MacKinnon's formulation, we can thus say that while no law gives white persons the express right to harm Black persons, this has not been necessary, since the law fails to prevent or address the harm suffered by Black persons, especially when this harm serves the interests of (white)

America.[229] Our laws are the fruit of a system designed to define and defend the ontological privilege of being unbranded. Our laws define and defend the right to subordinate persons of color. Our laws define and defend white supremacy.

While our laws purport to be for the people and by the people, because "person" means "white," as McWhorter explains, our laws' "most consistent effect is to promote the interests of the . . . Americans who, it so happens, own most of this country and its resources and assume they do so by biological and evolutionary right, by right of inheritance and by right of presumed fact that they are the most intelligent, most civilized, most morally upright people who ever lived."[230] The white right to harm Black persons is the sine qua non of white supremacy.[231] However, while Black persons need to watch every step within this per se dangerous and unfamiliar world,[232] white persons experience no such thing because, as Yancy notes, "their white bodies can move with ease, unraced, comfortable, and safe."[233] Black suffering thus becomes invisible and unintelligible to a white supremacist system that actually sees itself as largely colorblind and increasingly postracial.[234] The upshot, as Toni Morrison noted, is that "Americanness definitionally means whiteness," a tragic reality consistently confirmed.[235]

NOTES

1. Mills, *Racial Contract*, 111.

2. Yancy, *Black Bodies, White Gazes*, 11 (Our "racist historical system... has marked, and continues to mark, Black... life as devalued and nugatory."); see Zack, *White Privilege and Black Rights*, xvi (discussing the importance the Black-white dichotomy in contemporary America.)

3. Kant, Immanuel, "On The Different Human Races," trans. Jon Mark Mikkelsen in *Race and the Enlightenment: A Reader*, ed. Emmanuel Chukwudi Eze (Oxford: Wiley-Blackwell, 1997); Bowden, John, "Mitch McConnell sparks anger by saying Black Americans 'are voting in just as high a percentage as Americans,'" *Independent*, January 22, 2022.

4. Yancy, *Black Bodies, White Gazes*, 3; Ladelle McWhorter, "Racism and Biopower," in *On Race and Racism in America: Confessions in Philosophy*, ed. Roy Martinez (2010); Sara Ahmed "A Phenomenology of Whiteness," *Feminist Theory* 153 (2007).

5. Yancy, *Black Bodies, White Gazes*, 1 quoting West.

6. See, e.g., Andrade, Sofia, "'Y yo no me voy a quedar callado': Anti-Blackness and Colorism in Miami's Latinx Community," *Harvard Political Review*, August 10, 2020.

7. By American Latinidad I refer to the identity espoused by persons living in the United States who self-identify as Latinx or Hispanic. I specify the focus on the United States because people in Latin America generally do not consider themselves as belonging to a cohesive racial and/or political group.

8. Yancy, *Black Bodies, White Gazes*, 19 (discussing "darkness" as "a signifier of negative values grounded within a racist, social, and historical matrix.").

9. Ahmed, *Queer Phenomenology*, 129 (arguing that to be white is to be at home in the world); Manne, *Down Girl*, xiii (as regards gender privilege, arguing that men "tend to be subject to fewer social, moral, and legal constraints on their actions than their less privileged counterparts."). This does not imply that all white persons feel at home in the world by and for the unbranded. As discussed supra, a white person may well be subordinated by gender or class, for example. Qua white, however, a white person moves unencumbered in the world by and for whites.

10. Yancy, *Black Bodies, White Gazes*, 67; David Polizzi, *A Phenomenological Hermeneutic of Antiblack Racism in The Autobiography of Malcolm X* (Lanham: Lexington Books, 2019), 8.

11. Manne, *Down Girl*, xix; Yancy, *Black Bodies, White Gazes*, 81 ("To exist as Black is not to "stand out" facing an ontological horizon filled with future possibilities of being other than what one is." That is, "black" as defined by the white racist episteme.); Polizzi, *A Phenomenological Hermeneutic*, 10, 25.

12. Yancy, *Black Bodies, White Gazes*, 170, citing Toni Morrison, *The Bluest Eye*.

13. Polizzi, *A Phenomenological Hermeneutic*, 25. Cf Manne, *Down Girl*, 33.

14. Ahmed, *Queer Phenomenology*, 126.

15. Ahmed, *Queer Phenomenology*, 122; Polizzi, A Phenomenological Hermeneutic, 10.

16. Ahmed, *Queer Phenomenology*, 126.

17. Ahmed, *Queer Phenomenology*, 138.

18. Ahmed, *Queer Phenomenology*, 135.

19. Ahmed, *Queer Phenomenology*, 111.

20. Ahmed, *Queer Phenomenology*, 121.

21. Yancy, *Black Bodies, White Gazes*, xxxiv.

22. Cf. Mills, *Racial Contract*, 13, 80, 110; Taylor, J. *Techno-Racism: Heidegger's Philosophy of Technology and Critical Philosophies of Race* (Doctoral dissertation, Duquesne University) 2016. Much has been written on the Black-white binary, in particular with regards to the need for critical theory to move beyond it. The ontological model I propose here is helpful in this conversation by disclosing a fundamentally binary structure undergirding race (branded or unbranded) while creating space for exploring the phenomenologically rich worlds that each type of brandedness entails. Cf. *Society Must Be Defended*, 88 (discussing the binary nature of racism); McWhorter, *Racism and Sexual Oppression in Anglo-America*, 60 (discussing race as "a mechanism of power that proceeds or is guided by a logic that is executed in twos. The logic of race is a logic of a bifurcated social body.").

23. Ahmed, *Queer Phenomenology*, 122 (In this world, "whiteness is invisible and unmarked, as the absent center against which others appear only as deviants or as line of deviation."); Yancy, *Black Bodies, White Gazes*, 20 ("Whiteness is that according to which what is nonwhite is rendered other, marginal, ersatz, strange, native, inferior, uncivilized, and ugly."); Yancy, *Black Bodies, White Gazes*, 57 ("The surpluses whites gain... can be said to be ontological through existential exploitation."); Kendi, *Stamped from the Beginning*, 476 quoting x ("Race is not a biological

category that is politically charged. It is a political category that has been disguised as a biological one.")

24. Yancy, *Black Bodies, White Gazes*, 69.

25. MacKinnon, *Toward a Feminist Theory of the State*, 218; McWhorter, *Racism and Sexual Oppression in Anglo-America*, 58) (modern racism, quoting Foucault, "is not bound up with mentalities, ideologies, or the lies of power. It is bound up with the technique of power, with the technology of power.")

26. Yancy, *Black Bodies, White Gazes*, 189; Cf Foucault, *Society Must Be Defended*, 61 (discussing whiteness as "a race that is portrayed as the one true race, the race that holds power and is entitled to define the norm, and against those who deviate from that norm, against those who pose a threat to the biological heritage.")

27. Yancy, *Black Bodies, White Gazes*, 37.

28. Yancy, *Black Bodies, White Gazes*, 126 (arguing that whiteness is "an 'unconditioned' state of being. Acts of performing whiteness are interpreted both as... narrating one's being-in-the-world and as ways whites construct themselves as subjects in relation to those (in this case, Black bodies) who are thereby constructed as "things."'")

29. MacKinnon, *Toward a Feminist Theory of the State*, 241; cf. Manne, *Down Girl*, 29 (discussing how girls are "down-ranked or deprived").

30. Manne, *Down Girl*, 33 (discussing women's being in a "man's world"); Ahmed, *Queer Phenomenology*, 122; Yancy, *Black Bodies, White Gazes*, 37 ("Racism, properly understood, reduces Blacks below the human."); 81; 103 (The "white racist episteme... is a way of organizing the world politically, economically, and metaphysically."); Gary Peller, *Critical Race Consciousness* (Boulder: Paradigm Publishers, 2012), 15 (discussing the racial philosophies and ideologies operant "in the background of our social world.").

31. Ahmed, *Queer Phenomenology*, 111.

32. Cf. Yancy, *Black Bodies, White Gazes*, 223 (discussing how the white self is always already given as white: "the self is always already historically ensconced in frames of reference that render the social world intelligible and meaningful."); Zack, *White Privilege and Black Rights*, 6 (discussing the inculturation into racial norms through a "racial grammar... that structures cognition, vision, and even feelings on all sort of racial matters.").

33. Yancy, *Black Bodies, White Gazes*, 133 (arguing that "there is an invisible/imperceptible construction that occurs simultaneously with the process of white gazing. This construction does not involve 'seeing' the dark body and then extrapolating that it is inferior."); Alcoff, *Phenomenology of Racial Embodiment*, 184.

34. Michel Foucault, *Society Must Be Defended: Lectures at the College de France 1975-1976* (New York: Picador, 1997), 72.

35. Yancy, *Black Bodies, White Gazes*, 103.

36. Yancy, *Black Bodies, White Gazes*, 103 ("Black people have no role to play in 'the world of meaning as meaning-makers.'"); 144 (discussing Douglass seeing himself seen as something akin to a horse whose "existence was assigned a purpose by another, a white oppressor.").

37. Cf Kendi, *Stamped from the Beginning*, 18 (discussing that prejudice existed in the ancient world, but races did not).

38. Yancy, *Black Bodies, White Gazes*, 105.

39. As Toni Morrison recounts, "David Hume, Immanuel Kant and Thomas Jefferson, to mention only a few, had documented their conclusions that blacks were incapable of intelligence. Frederick Douglass knew otherwise, and he wrote refutations of what Jefferson said in 'Notes on the State of Virginia': 'Never yet could I find that a black had uttered a thought above the level of plain narration, never see even an elementary trait of painting or sculpture'—a sentence that I have always thought ought to be engraved at the door to the Rockefeller Collection of African Art. Hegel, in 1813, had said that Africans had no 'history' and couldn't write in modern languages. Kant disregarded a perceptive observation by a black man by saying, 'This fellow was quite black from head to foot, a clear proof that what he said was stupid.'" Morrison, *The Site of Memory*. See Mills, *Black Rights/ White Wrongs*, 95; Kendi, *Stamped from the Beginning*, 81.

40. McWhorter, *Racism and Sexual Oppression in Anglo-America*, 80; Kendi, *Stamped from the Beginning*, 82.

41. Mills, *Black Rights/ White Wrongs*, 95.

42. Mills, *Racial Contract*, 23, 56.

43. Mills, *Black Rights/ White Wrongs*, 62 (discussing the dehumanization of indigenous persons into "savages"), 99 (discussing Kant's equating humanity with whiteness), 107 (discussing how women and persons of color are seen as "intermediate creatures"—not fully human).

44. Mills, *Black Rights/ White Wrongs*, 92.

45. Mills, *Black Rights/ White Wrongs*, 92. See Kendi, *Stamped from the Beginning*, 82.

46. Mills, *Black Rights/ White Wrongs*, 124. Cf. McWhorter, *Racism and Sexual Oppression in Anglo-America*, 73 (discussing the transition of the concept of race from tribal/cultural to morphological).

47. Taylor, *Techno-Racism*, xxiii.

48. Sheth, *Toward a Political Philosophy of Race*; Taylor, *Techno-Racism*, 52.

49. Cf. Smith, David, "Paradoxes of Dehumanization," *Social Theory and Practice,* Jan. 16, p. 10.

50. Taylor, *Techno-Racism*, 13 (discussing the self-justifying nature of power).

51. Kendi, *Stamped from the Beginning*, 199.

52. Mills, *Racial Contract*, 32

53. Mills, *Racial Contract*, 16, 97; Mills, *Black Rights/ White Wrongs*, 93, 98; Kendi, *Stamped from the Beginning*, 56.

54. *Dred Scott v. Sandford*, 60 U.S. 393, 407 (1857).

55. See Cornel West, *Prophesy Deliverance: An Afro-American Revolutionary Christianity* (Louisville: Westminster John Knox Press, 1982).

56. Mills, *Racial Contract*, 3, 11; Mills, *Black Rights/ White Wrongs*, 37; Carol Pateman and Charles Mills, *Contract & Domination* (Cambridge: Polity, 2007).

57. For a critique of racial liberalism, see Mills, *Black Rights/ White Wrongs*, 23–29. Mills emphasizes the ideology inherent in opting for an ideal versus non-ideal

approach to ethical theory. Mills, *Black Rights/ White Wrongs*, 73. The ontological model I propose is consonant with what Mills describes as an "ideal-as-descriptive-model", *i.e.* an accurate model of how something actually works. Mills, *Black Rights/ White Wrongs*, 74.

58. Mills, *Racial Contract*, 12.

59. Carol Pateman, *The Sexual Contract* (Stanford: Stanford University Press, 1988).

60. Mills, *Black Rights/ White Wrongs*, 36. Regarding gender, see Pateman, *The Sexual Contract*; MacKinnon, *Toward a Feminist Theory of the State*, 229 ("To be a person, an abstract individual with abstract rights, may be a bourgeois concept, but its content is male.")

61. Mills, *Black Rights/ White Wrongs*, 36; Mills, *Racial Contract*, 98 (discussing epistemic bad faith as a component of the racial contract).

62. Pateman and Mills, *Contract & Domination*.

63. Mills, *Racial Contract*, 13.

64. Mills, *Racial Contract*, 11.

65. Mills, *Racial Contract*, 55.

66. Mills, *Black Rights/ White Wrongs*, 92 (arguing that "racism should be seen as a normative system in its own right that makes whiteness a prerequisite for full personhood and generally... limits nonwhites to 'sub-person' status.")

67. Mills, *Racial Contract*, 63; 58–59 (arguing that white exists only in juxtaposition with nonwhiteness "so that white self-conceptions of identity, personhood, and self-respect are then intimately tied up with the repudiation of the black Other."). Cf. Yancy, *Black Bodies, White Gazes*, 129 (discussing the "sociohistorical ontology of differences" presented as "natural through an ideology of whiteness.")

68. Mills, *Black Rights/ White Wrongs*, 47 (noting that white people's "favored status has meant that whites are commonly accepted as the 'normal' and norm-setting.").

69. Heidegger, *History of the Concept of Time*, 189; Yancy, *Black Bodies, White Gazes*, 10 (arguing that "Colonialism makes the world 'white.'").

70. The work of scholars such as Kendi and Jones helps disclose that racial subordination precedes ideological justification. Kendi, *Stamped from the Beginning*, 9–10 ("Racially discriminatory policies have usually sprung from economic, political, and cultural self-interests that are constantly changing."); 18 ("[h]ate and ignorance have not driven the history of racist ideas in America. Racist policies have driven the history of racist ideas in America."). In other words, persons were oppressed and ideas about race subsequently emerged to justify that oppression. Foucault's exhortation is instructive in this regard. Speaking of madness, he noted that "[i]f we concentrate on the techniques of power and show the economic profit or political utility that can be derived from them, in a certain context and for certain reasons, then we can understand how these mechanisms actually and eventually became part of the whole. In other words, the bourgeoisie doesn't give a damn about the mad, ... but it is interested in power over the mad." Foucault, *Society Must Be Defended*, 35. In MacKinnon's forceful formulation: "Inequality comes first; difference comes after. ... Difference is the velvet glove on the iron fist of domination." MacKinnon, *Toward a Feminist Theory of the State*, 219.

71. Kendi, *Stamped from the Beginning*; Mills, *Racial Contract*. Under the ontological brandedness model, the terms of domination contracts can be generalized into a brandedness contract under which members of society are heirs to the privileges of full personhood unless they bear the mark/s of subordinate persons.

72. McWhorter, *Racism and Sexual Oppression in Anglo-America*, 12.

73. McWhorter, *Racism and Sexual Oppression in Anglo-America*, 12 (noting that racism in 20th century Anglo-America had to be understood in light of Foucault's work on normalization), 221 (arguing that the so-called "moral defectives" of the early 20th century were seen as "defective" and thus "not truly human beings after all.").

74. Michel Foucault, *Abnormal: Lectures at the Collège de France 1974-1975*, trans. Graham Burchell (New York: Picador, 1999), 316–317. The passage quoted is followed by these lines: "It is a racism, therefore, whose function is not so much the prejudice or defense of one group against another as the detection of all those within a group who may be the carriers of a danger to it. It is an internal racism that permits the screening of every individual within a given society." When Foucault refers to a racism whose function is "the prejudice or defense of one group," he has in mind the battle between races that he describes at length in *Society Must Be Defended*. This is a struggle for power between groups on equal ontological footing. The racism of normalization, by contrast, is distinct in that it presumes that one group has won out in that battle. One group has become hegemonic in a culture and has become the norm. And the racism of normalization now functions to police that normality, detecting and addressing any threats to that normality. See McWhorter, *Racism and Sexual Oppression in Anglo-America*.

75. McWhorter, *Racism and Sexual Oppression in Anglo-America*, 140. McWhorter, following Foucault, argues that "[m]odern racism is about racial purification; it defines the abnormalities it identifies as racial impurities or as threats of racial impurity." *Racism and Sexual Oppression in Anglo-America*, 34. McWhorter is thus comfortable using the term "racism" as proxy for "actions taken in the betterment of the race," where such actions may be against persons of color or against queerness, for example.

76. Mills, *Black Rights/White Wrongs*, 114; Mills, *Racial Contract*, 20.

77. Mills takes a global view and does not limit his analysis to the U.S. He argues that white supremacy is a global political system, of which the U.S. is but one example. Mills, *Black Rights/ White Wrongs*, 152 (arguing that the mythos of the American founding is "a triumph of intellectual evasion achieved by utilizing orthodox class categories imported across the Atlantic and ignoring the emergence in the New World of a *new kind* of ascriptive social hierarchy: race.").

78. Mills, *Black Rights/ White Wrongs*, 41 ("The opposition between white and nonwhite has been foundational to the workings of American social and political institutions.").

79. James Baldwin, *I Am Not Your Negro*, ed. Raoul Peck (Paris: R. Laffont, 2017), 95.

80. Kendi, *Stamped from the Beginning*; Jacqueline Jones, *A Dreadful Deceit: The Myth of Race from the Colonial Era to Obama's America* (New York: Basic Books, 2013).

81. Kendi, *Stamped from the Beginning*, 38.
82. Jones, *A Dreadful Deceit*, 7.
83. McWhorter, *Racism and Sexual Oppression in Anglo-America*, 66.
84. Yancy, *Black Bodies, White Gazes*, 130.
85. Ta-Nehisi Coates, *Between the World and Me* (New York: Spiegel & Grau, 2015), 102.
86. Yancy, *Black Bodies, White Gazes*, 130.
87. Jones, *A Dreadful Deceit*, 44.
88. Jones, *A Dreadful Deceit*, 44.
89. Jones, *A Dreadful Deceit*, 44; McWhorter, *Racism and Sexual Oppression in Anglo-America*, 70.
90. Calvin Warren, *Ontological Terror: Blackness, Nihilism, and Emancipation* (Durham: Duke University Press, 2018), 52, 65, 74 (discussing Black being as tool for whiteness).
91. McWhorter, *Racism and Sexual Oppression in Anglo-America*, 73–74.
92. Following Gary Peller, I will define privilege as the right to harm. See Gary Peller, *Privilege* 104 Geo. L. J. 883–920 (2016), 885. (arguing, via Oliver Wendell Holmes, that "the law acts to create a privilege on the part of one private party any time it declines to recognize a right on the part of another to recover for harm inflicted by the first."). Peller's work also problematizes the public-private distinction which lies at the heart of the contemporary jurisprudence that has shaped our approach to race and racial justice. Peller, *Privilege* 899; Peller, *Critical Race Consciousness*, 124. Cf. Kendi, *Stamped from the Beginning*, 372 (discussing a "freedom to oppress").
93. In 1630 a white man was whipped in Virginia for "defiling his body by laying with a negro." Kendi, *Stamped from the Beginning*, 39. But in 1649 an interracial couple punished for fornication in Virginia received the same punishment as white-white fornicating couples, in the 1650's half of Black planters in eastern Virginia married white wives, and in 1654 Black and white fornicating couples in Virginia received the same punishment, McWhorter, *Racism and Sexual Oppression in Anglo-America*, 71.
94. McWhorter, *Racism and Sexual Oppression in Anglo-America*, 72, 344n20.
95. McWhorter, *Racism and Sexual Oppression in Anglo-America*, 66.
96. McWhorter, *Racism and Sexual Oppression in Anglo-America*, 75.
97. McWhorter, *Racism and Sexual Oppression in Anglo-America*, 72.
98. McWhorter, *Racism and Sexual Oppression in Anglo-America*, 75.
99. McWhorter, *Racism and Sexual Oppression in Anglo-America*, 76.
100. McWhorter, *Racism and Sexual Oppression in Anglo-America*, 69.
101. Kendi, *Stamped from the Beginning*, 41.
102. McWhorter, *Racism and Sexual Oppression in Anglo-America*, 69–70.
103. Kendi, *Stamped from the Beginning*, 49; McWhorter, *Racism and Sexual Oppression in Anglo-America*, 344.
104. Kendi, *Stamped from the Beginning*, 41; McWhorter, *Racism and Sexual Oppression in Anglo-America*, 69.
105. Kendi, *Stamped from the Beginning*, 41; McWhorter, *Racism and Sexual Oppression in Anglo-America*, 71.

106. Kendi, *Stamped from the Beginning*, 53; McWhorter, *Racism and Sexual Oppression in Anglo-America*, 71.

107. Kendi, *Stamped from the Beginning*, 53.

108. McWhorter, *Racism and Sexual Oppression in Anglo-America*, 76.

109. Kendi, *Stamped from the Beginning*, 68; McWhorter, Racism and Sexual Oppression in Anglo-America, 74.

110. McWhorter, *Racism and Sexual Oppression in Anglo-America*, 73.

111. MacKinnon, *Toward a Feminist Theory of the State*, 245.

112. McWhorter, *Racism and Sexual Oppression in Anglo-America*, 76.

113. Isenberg, *White Trash*, 264.

114. Kendi, *Stamped from the Beginning*, 54.

115. The Racial Contract reconciles the contradiction between egalitarianism and slavery. Mills, *Racial Contract*, 64. To the framers, non-Europeans were "non-peoples". Mills, *Racial Contract*, 28.

116. Mills, *Black Rights/White Wrongs*, 62.

117. Yancy, *Black Bodies, White Gazes*, xxxi. For related discussions of biopower, see Sheth, *Toward a Political Philosophy of Race*; McWhorter, *Racism and Sexual Oppression in Anglo-America*.

118. Kendi, *Stamped from the Beginning*, 123.

119. See Kendi, *Stamped from the Beginning*, 173–174 ("After Turner's rebellion, Virginians started seriously contemplating the end of slavery. It was not from the moral persuasion of nonviolent abolitionists, but from the fear of slave revolts, or the 'smothered volcano' that could one day kill them all. During the winter of 1831–1832, undercover abolitionists, powerful colonizationists, and hysterical legislators in Virginia raised their voices against slavery. In the end, proslavery legislators batted away every single antislavery measure, and ended up pushing through an even more harrowing slave code than the one that had been in place. Proslavery legislators repressed the very captives they said were docile, and restricted the education of the very people they argued could not be educated. Racist ideas, clearly, did not generate these slave codes. Enslaving interests generated these slave codes. Racist ideas were produced to preserve the enslaving interests."); Warren, *Ontological Terror*, 53 (discussing the ontological terror whiteness experiences when the color boundaries are challenged).

120. Kendi, *Stamped from the Beginning*, 123.

121. *Dred Scott v. Sandford*, 60 U.S. 393, 407 (1857).

122. Calvin Warren, *Ontological Terror*, 49.

123. Coates, *Between the World and Me*, 104; 32 ("The power of domination and exclusion is central to the belief in being white, and without it, 'white people' would cease to exist for want of reasons."); Linda Martín Alcoff, *The Future of Whiteness* (Cambridge: Polity, 2015).

124. Cheryl Harris, "Whiteness as Property," 106 *Harvard L. Rev.* 8 (June 1993).

125. Peller, "Privilege," 896 ("Every right to property entails a corresponding duty on the part of others not to use the property, in contrast to the nonregulation imagery of private property discourse.").

126. McWhorter, *Racism and Sexual Oppression in Anglo-America*, 77; Kendi, *Stamped from the Beginning*, 74 (describing the 18th century "Christian" slave-owner

ideology under which "the Golden Rule did not suggest equality between 'superiors and inferiors.'... [Masters] were to baptize and treat their slaves kindly.").

127. Warren, *Ontological Terror*, 81.

128. Peller, *Critical Race Consciousness*, 37.

129. *Plessy v. Ferguson*, 163 U.S. 537, 544 (1896). Regarding segregation in the North, see, e.g. Kendi, *Stamped from the Beginning*, 356–357; Rothstein, *Color of Law*, 40; Polizzi, *A Phenomenological Hermeneutic*, 24.

130. Kendi, *Stamped from the Beginning*, 259 ("Hate fueled the lynching era. But behind this hatred lay racist ideas that had evolved to question Black freedoms at every stage. And behind these racist ideas were powerful White men, striving by word and deed to regain absolute political, economic, and cultural control of the South. This corresponds to the policing of ontological boundaries."). Cf. Manne, *Down Girl*.

131. McWhorter, *Racism and Sexual Oppression in Anglo-America*, 158–159; Coates, *Between the World and Me*, 60 ("Hate gives identity. The nigger, the fag, the bitch illuminate the border, illuminate what we ostensibly are not, illuminate the Dream of being white, of being a Man. We name the hated strangers and are thus confirmed in the tribe."). Compare with Nietzsche's reflection on the beautiful and the ugly, the latter being a "value judgment" through which "[a] hatred is aroused—but whom does man hate then? There is no doubt: the decline of his type. Here he hates out of the deepest instinct of the species; in this hatred there is a shudder, caution, depth, farsightedness—it is the deepest hatred there is." "Twilight of the Idols," in *The Portable Nietzsche*, ed. Walter Kaufmann (New York: Penguin, 1982), 527. See Kate Manne, "In Ferguson and Beyond, Punishing Humanity," *NYT* (October 12, 2014); Sheth, *Toward a Political Philosophy of Race* (discussing unruliness); Warren, *Ontological Terror*, 107.

132. Allison Keyes, "A Long-Lost Manuscript Contains a Searing Eyewitness Account of the Tulsa Race Massacre of 1921," *smithsonianmag.com* (May 27, 2016).

133. Allison Keyes, "A Long-Lost Manuscript Contains a Searing Eyewitness Account of the Tulsa Race Massacre of 1921," *smithsonianmag.com* (May 27, 2016); Alexandra Natapoff, *Punishment Without Crime: How our Massive Misdemeanor System Traps the Innocent and Makes America more Unequal* (New York: Basic Books, 2018), 174.

134. MacKinnon, *Toward a Feminist Theory of the State*, 245 (emphasis added); Manne, *Down Girl*.

135. See Richard Rothstein, *The Color of Law* (New York: Liveright Publishing, 2017) (detailing the ways in which U.S. law systematically centered the interests of whiteness through affirmative government programs that purposefully excluded persons of color, especially Black persons); Peller, *Critical Race Consciousness*, 75.

136. Yancy, *Black Bodies, White Gazes*, 177.

137. Peller, *Critical Race Consciousness*, xiv.

138. Mills, *Racial Contract*, 73 (discussing that the Racial Contract is formally abolished but lives on de facto); Kendi, *Stamped from the Beginning*, 362 (discussing the racism underlying Warren's opinion that "separate Black educational facilities were inherently unequal and inferior because Black students were not being exposed to White students." That is, Black students were being deprived the opportunity to

develop fully and allow the meaninglessness of blackness to disappear); Polizzi, *A Phenomenological Hermeneutic*, 119; Taylor, *Techno-Racism*, 41 (discussing how racism has not disappeared but transformed).

139. Of course, this contemporary version of King, with its "emphasis on nonviolence hides [the] power/confrontation dimension of King's organizing and tends to make invisible the threat to fundamental power relations manifest in the mass organizing of the Black community during the civil rights mobilizations." Peller, *Critical Race Consciousness*, 44.

140. López, Ian Haney, "Race and Colorblindness after *Hernandez* and *Brown*," 25 *Chicana/o Latina/o L. Rev.* 1 (2005).

141. See Peller, *Critical Race Consciousness*, xii (arguing that mainstream "integrationist" American notions "locat[e] racial oppression in the social structure of prejudice and stereotype based on skin color and . . . identif[y] progress with the transcendence of a racial consciousness about the world."), 22–23, 51("race consciousness [as] the very definition of racial oppression.").

142. Manne, *Down Girl*, 18.

143. Kendi, *Stamped from the Beginning*, 9.

144. See Peller, *Critical Race Consciousness*, xii ("Along with the suppression of white racism that was the widely celebrated aim of civil rights reform, the dominant conception of racial justice was framed to require that Black nationalism be equated with white supremacy and that race consciousness on the part of either whites or Blacks be marginalized as beyond the good sense of "enlightened" American culture."), 22–23; Mills, *Black Rights/ White Wrongs*, 56 (discussing theories under which Black people are superior to white people); Kendi, *Stamped from the Beginning*, 396 (Vice President Hubert Humphrey explained in 1966 that "racism is racism—and there is no room in America for racism of any color."), 452 (discussing Bill Clinton's "assimilationist maneuver of equating antiracists with segregationists").

145. *Adarand v. Peña*, 515 US 200 (1995).

146. *Parents Involved*, 551 US 701 (2007).

147. *Schuette v. Coalition to Defend Affirmative Action*, 572 US 291 (2014).

148. *Adarand* 206.

149. *Adarand* 205, 208.

150. *Adarand* 205.

151. *Adarand* 205–206, 210.

152. *Adarand* 237.

153. *Adarand* 214, quoting *Hirabayashi*.

154. *Adarand* 229–230.

155. *Adarand* 224, quoting *Bakke*.

156. *Adarand* 227.

157. *Adarand* 227.

158. Peller, *Critical Race Consciousness*, 67.

159. *Adarand* 239.

160. *Adarand* 239.

161. *Adarand* 239. Cf. Manne, *Down Girl*, 32.

162. *Adarand* 239.

163. *Adarand* 239.
164. *Adarand* 240.
165. *Adarand* 240.
166. *Adarand* 241.
167. *Adarand* 229.
168. *Adarand* 270.
169. *Adarand* 275.
170. Cf. Alcoff, *Visible Identities*, 183–184; Alcoff, *Towards a Phenomenology of Racial Embodiment*, 189; Dembroff, "Real Talk on the Metaphysics of Gender," 24.
171. Kendi, *Stamped from the Beginning*, 385.
172. *Parents Involved in Community Schools v. Seattle School District No. 1*, 551 US 701, 712 (2007).
173. *Parents Involved* 716.
174. *Parents Involved* 714–715, 717–718.
175. *Parents Involved* 723.
176. *Parents Involved* 749.
177. *Parents Involved* 712
178. Rothstein, *Color of Law*, 138.
179. *Parents Involved* 730. Internal citations omitted.
180. *Parents Involved* 748.
181. Mills, *Black Rights/White Wrongs*, 34–35.
182. Patricia J. Williams, *The Alchemy of Race and Rights: Diary of a Law Professor* (Cambridge: Harvard University Press, 1991), 116.
183. E.g., John Powell, "Parents involved: the Mantle of Brown, the Shadow of Plessy," 46 *U. Louisville L. Rev.* 631 (2008); Ronald Turner, "*Plessy* 2.0," 13 *Lewis & Clark L. Rev.* 861 - 919 (Winter 2009); Jack Balkin and Reva Siegel, eds., "Remembering How to Do Equality," in *The Constitution in 2020* (Oxford: Oxford University Press, 2020); López, Ian Haney," Race And Colorblindness After *Hernandez* and *Brown*," 25 *Chicana/o Latina/o L. Rev.* 1 (2005); Joel K. Goldstein, "Not Hearing History: A Critique of Chief Justice Roberts's Reinterpretation of Brown," 69 *Ohio State L. J.* 791 (2008).
184. Cf. Polizzi, *A Phenomenological Hermeneutic*, 3 (discussing the ways in which Black communities are blamed for their own conditions); Kendi, *Stamped from the Beginning*, 166 ("America's favorite racist pastime: denying Blacks access to education and jobs and then calling their resultant impoverished state 'natural'").
185. Cf. Peller, *Privilege* 916. ("From the baseline definition of unconstitutional discrimination as limited to intentional or purposeful discrimination, affirmative action appears as the government intervening in the results of an otherwise racially neutral realm."); 915 ("It is analytically no more coherent to see affirmative action as the introduction of racial criteria into a formerly aracial, neutral baseline than it is to see the failure to engage in affirmative action as the privileging of social practices that distribute burdens disproportionately by race.").
186. Peller, *Privilege* 918 (This "'essential dichotomy' between public and private acts" reflects the contemporary situation of mainstream legal discourse in which it is

intellectually respectable to rely on the traditional liberal construction of the public and private"); 896 ("Private coercion depends on public power.").

187. *Plessy v. Ferguson*, 163 U.S. 537, 551 (1896) ("We consider the underlying fallacy of the plaintiff's argument to consist in the assumption that the enforced separation of the two races stamps the colored race with a badge of inferiority. If this be so, it is not by reason of anything found in the act, but solely because the colored race chooses to put that construction upon it.").

188. Mills, *Racial Contract*, 77 (noting that by regarding the status quo as a "somehow neutral baseline,… the idealized social contract renders permanent the legacy of the Racial Contract.").

189. *Parents Involved* 722.

190. *Schuette* 299.

191. *Schuette* 301.

192. *Schuette* 307 (rejecting the idea that "any state action with a "racial focus" that makes it "more difficult for certain racial minorities than for other groups" to "achieve legislation that is in their interest" is subject to strict scrutiny.").

193. Jack Balkin and Reva Siegel, eds., "Remembering How to Do Equality," in *The Constitution in 2020* (Oxford: Oxford University Press, 2020), 102 ("Increasingly equality doctrine does not prevent law from maintaining social caste; it prevents governments from remedying and dismantling caste.")

194. Balkin and Siegel, "Remembering How to Do Equality," 106.

195. Hull, Gordon "Equitable Relief as a Relay Between Juridical and Biopower: The Case of School Desegregation" 50 *G. Cont. Philos. Rev.* 225 (2017); Yancy, *Black Bodies, White Gazes*, 224 (discussing importance of a multicultural environment because "transacting with flesh and blood bodies of color can function as a powerful catalyst that can trigger an ambush" on whiteness).

196. Andrew Chung et al, "Shielded: For Cops Who Kill, Special Supreme Court Protection," *Reuters Investigates* (8 May 2020).

197. Rothstein, *Color of Law*.

198. Natapoff, *Punishment Without Crime*.

199. Alexander, *The New Jim Crow*; Yancy, *Black Bodies, White Gazes*, 33. See Mills, *Black Rights/ White Wrongs*, 42 for a list of things still wrong; Manne, *Down Girl*, 4, 11; Rothstein, *Color of Law*; E. Girvan and H. J. Marek, "Psychological and Structural Bias in Civil Jury Awards," 8 *J. Aggress. Conflict Peace Res.* 4 (2016): 247–257; Ronen Avraham and Kimberly Yuracko, "Torts and Discrimination," 78 *Ohio St. L. J.* (2017); Wriggins, Jennifer "Tort, Race, and the Value of Injury: 1900-1949," 49 *How. L. J.* 99 (2005).

200. Coates, *Between the World and Me*, 102.

201. McWhorter, *Racism and Sexual Oppression in Anglo-America*, 168; Alexander, *The New Jim Crow*; Natapoff, *Punishment Without Crime*; Sheth, *Toward a Political Philosophy of Race*.

202. Coates, *Between the World and Me*, 101; Zack, *White Privilege and Black Rights*; Alexander, *The New Jim Crow*; Natapoff, *Punishment Without Crime*.

203. Coates, *Between the World and Me*, 78.

204. Nicholas Bogel-Burroughs, "What We Learned on Day 2 of the Derek Chauvin Trial" *NYT* March 30, 2021.

205. Jennifer De Pinto, "CBS News Poll: Widespread Agreement with Chauvin Verdict." *CBS News* April 25, 2021.

206. For more on qualified immunity, see the Equal Justice Initiative at https://eji.org/issues/qualified-immunity/. As the Equal Justice Initiative explains, "Americans were first empowered to challenge police misconduct in 1871, when Congress passed a law allowing lawsuits against state and local authorities who refused to protect African Americans from—or even participated in—racial terror lynchings and other acts of racial violence by groups like the Ku Klux Klan." Through its doctrine of qualified immunity, however, the Supreme Court has effectively created an absolute shield against accountability for police officers accused of using excessive force.

207. "Interview: George Zimmerman breaks silence on 'Hannity,'" *Fox News Channel*. July 18, 2012. At https://video.foxnews.com/v/1741879195001#sp=show-clips. Note that George Zimmerman's background is multiracial such that his appearance would not permit him to be considered white in much of United States. That being said, Zimmerman effectively *became* white when attention turned to him vis-à-vis Martin.

208. Polizzi, *A Phenomenological Hermeneutic*, 3.

209. Yancy, *Black Bodies, White Gazes*, 3.

210. Kendi, *Stamped from the Beginning*, 156. Cf. Natapoff, *Punishment Without Crime*, 20.

211. Yancy, *Black Bodies, White Gazes*, 74 (discussing that "white acceptance comes at an existential ontological price for Black people: a mode of nonbeing"); 170 (discussing Morrison's *The Bluest Eye*, where the salvation of blue eyes equals psychological death).

212. Coates, *Between the World and Me*, 93–95. Compare with Ellison's *Invisible Man*, 4, when the white man refuses to apologize for insulting him. Cf. Natapoff, *Punishment Without Crime*, 160.

213. Yancy, *Black Bodies, White Gazes*, 22.

214. Zack, *White Privilege and Black Rights*, 58; Alexander, *The New Jim Crow*; Natapoff, *Punishment Without Crime*.

215. Zack, *White Privilege and Black Rights*, 75. Regarding white innocence, consider Yancy's discussion of the 2006 Jena High School incident in Jena, Louisiana, where Black students protested segregation by sitting under a tree that was defacto for white students only. The following day, three nooses were found hanging from the tree. The incident was dismissed by the school and the board of education as "a youthful prank." Yancy, *Black Bodies, White Gazes*, Xxxi; McWhorter, *Racism and Sexual Oppression in Anglo-America*, 213; Natapoff, *Punishment Without Crime*, 168; Morrison, Steven R. "Will to Power..." *Northwestern J. L. Soc. Pol.* (2007).

216. Yancy, *Black Bodies, White Gazes*, xxxv.

217. Yancy, *Black Bodies, White Gazes*, xxx.

218. Coates, *Between the World and Me*; Baldwin, *I Am Not Your Negro*; du Bois, *Souls of Black Folk*; Yancy, *Black Bodies, White Gazes*, xxx, 88.

219. Zack, *White Privilege and Black Rights*, 69.

220. Zack, *White Privilege and Black Rights*, 69.

221. Yancy, *Black Bodies, White Gazes*, 33.

222. Coates, Ta-Nehisi, "Trayvon Martin and the Irony of American Justice," *The Atlantic* (15 July 2013).

223. Yancy, *Black Bodies, White Gazes*, 5.

224. Yancy, *Black Bodies, White Gazes*, 7.

225. Warren, *Ontological Terror*, 54.

226. For an extended discussion of the one, see Dreyfus, *Being-in-the-World*, 151 et seq; Heidegger, *Being and Time*, 163 et seq; Heidegger, *Ontology*, 65. Consider how different this experience of the collective one is for the unbranded, for whom the dissolution into the norm is markedly different than for the branded, for whom dissolution into the norm of humanity is impossible, and for whom dissolution instead implies acquiescing to the roles permitted the branded. Mills, *Black Rights/ White Wrongs*, 54 quoting Du Bois ("Correspondingly, the 'central metaphor' of W.E.B. Du Bois's *The Souls of Black Folk* is the image of the 'veil,' and the Black American cognitive equivalent of the shocking moment of Cartesian realization of the uncertainty of everything one had taken to be knowledge is the moment when for Du Bois, as a child in New England, 'it dawned upon me with a certain suddenness that I was different from the others; or like, mayhap, in heart and life and longing, but shut out from their world by a vast veil.'").

227. Polizzi, *A Phenomenological Hermeneutic*, 6 (discussing the whiteness of the they-self); Yancy, *Black Bodies, White Gazes*, 5, 66; Zack, *White Privilege and Black Rights*, 90; Taylor J 53.

228. Warren, *Ontological Terror*; Yancy, *Black Bodies, White Gazes*; Frantz Fanon, *Black Skin, White Masks* (New York: Grove Press, 1952).

229. MacKinnon, *Toward a Feminist Theory of the State*, 239. Consider Coates' question as he learned history in school: "Why were only our heroes nonviolent?" Coates, *Between the World and Me*, 32; Peller, *Critical Race Consciousness*, 74 (regarding practices that demonstrate "disparate real world-power regardless of the legal form" taken.)

230. McWhorter, *Racism and Sexual Oppression in Anglo-America*, 290 (discussing the context of so-called family values,); see Coates, *Between the World and Me*, 32 (""White America" is a syndicate arrayed to protect its exclusive power to dominate and control our bodies. Sometimes this power is direct (lynching), and sometimes it is insidious (redlining). But however it appears, the power of domination and exclusion is central to the belief in being white, and without it, "white people" would cease to exist for want of reasons.")

231. Coates, *Between the World and Me*, 104.

232. Coates, *Between the World and Me*; Natapoff, *Punishment Without Crime*; Alexander, *The New Jim Crow*; Mitchell, Sarah, "Theorizing Mass Incarceration: Augmenting Foucault," *OSWEGO* (2014).

233. Yancy, *Black Bodies, White Gazes*, 9.

234. Yancy, *Black Bodies, White Gazes*, 66–67 (discussing the unintelligibility of Black suffering to white eyes); MacKinnon, *Toward a Feminist Theory of the State*, 215.

235. Mills, *Racial Contract*, 58 quoting Morrison. *See, e.g.*, John Bowden, "Mitch McConnell sparks anger by saying Black Americans 'are voting in just as high a percentage as Americans'" *Independent* January 22, 2022.

Chapter 4

The Pale and Inconspicuous Presence

The ontological model of race reveals the mechanisms by which U.S. law moved from a place where servitude was untethered to race, to one where slavery was racial per se, to one of de jure racial discrimination, to the current one where race continues to relegate people to a permanent subordinate ontological category despite a formally colorblind legal system. Because race is a tool to subordinate persons of color in order to privilege whiteness, race is ultimately not about the constellation of facts that land us with a particular racial label but about our distinct ways of being (allowed to be) in the world. While recognizing that race is a social construction imposed to manufacture distinctions between otherwise equivalent entities, we can nonetheless see how race is a real tool in the real world that creates and maintains a whiteness and nonwhiteness that are real and unequal. By now passing race off as an insignificant constellation of mere facts, U.S. law conceals the tool nature of race and normalizes ontological inequalities, so that white privilege and nonwhite subordination simply fade into the pale and inconspicuous presence of the (white) world.

By branding certain persons as subordinate in order to privilege the unbranded as persons simpliciter, race is inherently about creating and maintaining ontological inequalities. The ways of being in the world available to you are in significant part determined by your race. As a person simpliciter, a white person is ontologically free to embody nearly limitless ways of being within a (white) world built around individual equality and freedom. By contrast, a person of color, especially a Black person, is branded an in-order-to-serve and is ontologically restricted to only certain permissible ways of being in that (white) world. The being of white persons thus gets to unfurl freely, unencumbered as it moves through its familiar world, while the being of persons of color is constrained, encumbered by the brand that designates the bearer as ontologically subordinate and thus disqualified from full participation in the (white) world.

Within a white world, persons of color and white persons are not ontological equals, and this inequality results in concrete, tangible privileges white persons enjoy at the expense of persons of color. Accordingly, turning a blind eye to race for the sake of equality entirely misses the source of inequality and guarantees that inequality can never meaningfully be addressed. Instead, as I will argue in Chapter 5, racial equality is best understood in terms of ontological equality, and racial justice is best framed as dismantling ontological subordination and privilege. Understanding race as an ontological brand helps us keep our focus on the power inequality inherent in race.

Contemporary (white) America is simultaneously structured around the liberalist credo of all persons being infinitely and equally valuable and structured in a way that distinguishes between who gets to be considered a person simpliciter and who does not. Our state of ontological brandedness determines the state of our personhood and defines the ways of being we are permitted to embody. To be branded means that the world is on notice that the bearer of the brand is not supposed to participate in this world as a person simpliciter. The branded are instead supposed to participate in the world in the subordinate role proper to them given the particular type of demoted person they are. The branded are, to use Yancy's words, "ontologically closed."[1] By comparison, the roles available to the unbranded are virtually unrestricted, and ontological openness becomes part of the spoils of privilege.

The brand of race enables us to publicly display for one another the racial type of things we are and where we are supposed to be within this racialized social system. A white person is ontologically unbranded and thus able to fulfill any number of roles. But someone branded as nonwhite, especially someone branded with blackness, is supposed to remain within the supporting roles permitted to subordinate persons. If they do, they largely fade into the invisible background of (white) America; if they step beyond those confines, however, they are foregrounded and become obtrusive. When we go to the movies and see a boy meets girl movie, the vast majority of the time it is a white boy meeting a white girl. If it is a Black boy meeting a Black girl, it ceases to be just a story and becomes a Black story. If it is a white boy meeting a Black girl or a Black girl meeting a white boy, it becomes a story about race, not just a story. And so, when we have the opioid epidemic, it is an epidemic because it is affecting "us," i.e., We the People, i.e., white people. But when it largely affects Black people, it is not really affecting "us," and it is not a problem as such, but a *Black* problem. There is, in fact, no such thing as a white problem—there are just problems—because the white world is in fact the world, i.e., (white) America. But Black problems arise in the Black world, which does not get to be part of (white) America. People can thus theorize as to why "those blacks" have "those problems," but at the end of the day, they are not "our" problems. This dynamic results in what Yancy has called "white ethical solipsism."[2]

Race is a tool and, as such, exists within a totality of references, a referential whole that defines the set of tools and the know-how needed to do its work, viz., the work of ontologically subordinating the branded to privilege the unbranded.[3] Within this racialized world, there are roles open for white persons—the protagonists of the white world—and roles permitted persons of color—supporting roles in the white world. Brands allow us to look at a person and make an immediate and preconscious assessment of their ontological status. When we come upon someone new, we are able to make an immediate determination regarding whether this person bears a brand and, if so, of what type. It is analogous to simultaneously asking for and receiving someone's ontological papers. From that initial moment, our comportment toward that person is informed by that person's ontological status.[4] Whiteness enjoys the treatment due to a person simpliciter, while those that bear racial brands are relegated to subordinate castes. Because the use of this tool is endemic to and universal in our culture, we learn to use it at an early age, and it quickly withdraws into the invisible background of our everyday practices.[5] The result is that because the brand of race and its use are intimately familiar to us, so much a part of everyday American life, our everyday treatment of the branded as subordinate is largely hidden from conscious view for most of us.[6] A white person's own unbrandedness is particularly inconspicuous because it is very difficult to see ones' own lack of abnormality.[7]

This invisibility is the evidence of our know-how, of our mastery of the tools needed to move familiarly within our world. The mechanics of race are invisible to us the way, for example, rules governing personal space are invisible. Nevertheless, like other tools rendered invisible by familiarity, the tool-nature of race can be made conspicuous by studying breakdown cases. In a manner similar to how we might be chatting away, absorbed in a party, not even aware that there is such a thing as personal space or social roles until another guest stands too close to comfortably speak with, or we see a server comfortably eating from the buffet, the tool-nature of race can be seen in situations where race fails to do its intended work of clearly identifying subordinate persons.[8]

RACING, ONTOLOGICAL SUBORDINATION, AND ONTOLOGICAL PRIVILEGE

Ontological brands designate the bearers as ontologically subordinate to the unbranded. In the United States, the brand of race designates persons of color as ontologically subordinate to white persons. The brand of race works because it is a visible sign universally recognized in (white) America. Members of this (white) world learn to use the tool of race in the everyday practice of racing, that is, the process by which we determine whether someone is a white person (person simpliciter) or a person of color (subordinated person).

The mechanics of ontological brandedness unfold in a largely invisible manner because race is a familiar tool we use in the course of ordinary everydayness. When the brand of race works as it is supposed to, our use of the tool of race becomes inconspicuous, and racing, instead of being a conscious activity, becomes simply the preconscious determination of someone as white or nonwhite (and if nonwhite, what type) that then informs our comportment toward that person.[9] But the inconspicuousness of a familiar tool breaks down when it fails to perform its function. Because an ontological brand is a visible sign that serves to distinguish between the branded and the unbranded, the brand fails to perform its function if it fails to clearly designate the branded as such. Under these circumstances, the determination of a person's racial status goes from preconscious to conscious, and we find the question of that person's racial designation very much in the foreground of our experience.

Consider the drive so many of us feel to find out "what" someone is when their racial designation is unclear. If we are unclear regarding a person's racial background, many of us feel discomfort.[10] Where are they from? This is particularly salient for people whose skin color is light but, to the common American eye, seems "exotic" or "ethnic" in some way. If someone is not easily categorized as white or nonwhite, we want to know *what* that person *is*. But what something *is* is inextricable from what it is *for*. In Heidegger's words, when we come across something "strange... the question 'what is it' explicates itself into a 'What is it for? What are we supposed to do with it?'"[11] If white, i.e., if unbranded, then the person before us is a person simpliciter to be treated as such. If nonwhite, i.e., if branded, however, then the person before us is a subordinated person permissibly treated as an in-order-to-serve. Ambiguity in brandedness brings the usually preconscious determination of brandedness into our consciousness. As it works with race, so does it work with gender, where, for example, it is very unsettling to many if a person's gender is ambiguous. These are categories that many of us want to be very clearly defined. We want to be able to categorize someone as man or woman, as white or nonwhite, in order to make that all-important determination: person simpliciter or not?

It may be argued that this is just a natural reaction to otherness, that we humans have natural tribal instincts, that we are aware of the difference, and that we fear the unknown. Because we fear what is different from us, the drive to find out "what" someone is would be equally present if we came across a group of Norwegian speakers, for example. It is simple curiosity. But the empirical evidence demonstrates that this is not a curiosity with power-neutral implications. If my new colleague has a funny accent, and I ask where they're from, and it turns out to be Norway, it has little bearing on anything because the funny accent corresponds to a power-neutral strangeness; we do not ontologically demote Norwegians.[12] Racing, by contrast, is not a power-neutral phenomenon. Racing is an activity essential to the policing of the boundary between the privileged and the subordinated.[13] Because our curiosity about ambiguous racial determinations is always operating within a world where a person of color does not enjoy full access to the rights and privileges afforded a white person, our curiosity about race is curiosity about the rules of applicable engagement vis-à-vis this person before me.[14]

In (white) America, the brand of race—particularly the brand of blackness—marks one for exclusion from the rights and privileges afforded full personhood. Black persons are epistemically suspect. Black suffering is valued less than white suffering. Black persons are considered less evolved than white persons. As implicit bias research has helped confirm, the devaluation of persons of color, especially of Black persons, is normal and invisible.[15] Further, the ontological subordination of blackness and the concomitant privileging of whiteness is endemic not only to whiteness but to the white *world*, a world we all inhabit. It is not the case that members of a particular racial group simply favor members of their same group; instead, the bearers of brands are subordinated while the unbranded are privileged by the branded and unbranded alike. An endemic antiblack bias exists not only among white persons, but also among people of color, including Black persons.[16]

This general devaluation of the lives of persons branded as nonwhite is the ontological violence at the heart of racial injustice.[17] Within (white) America, a white person, qua person simpliciter, is generally valued in terms of *who* that person is, and because, in Heideggerian terms, a person's essence is their existence, to truly know a person we must know their ways of being in the world. But Black persons do not enjoy this same treatment. In (white) America, the brand of blackness deprives the bearer of the identity of essence and existence and instead reduces the bearer to an entity with, in Yancy's words, "an essence (Blackness) that precedes [their] existence."[18] Importantly, this essence does not correspond to blackness as defined by the lived experiences of Black persons; instead, the content of this imposed blackness is determined by the subordinating power of the (white) world that unfolds to preserve and advance the interests of white supremacy. It is through this process of seeing the brand of blackness and having that brand devalue and predetermine who the bearer is that, as Yancy puts it, "Black bodies are constituted through a racist episteme, a way of 'knowing' in advance."[19]

Within the ordinary everydayness of (white) America, the brand of blackness preconsciously attributes to the bearer an essence of blackness determined by a racist episteme. Given the ontological power wielded by a hegemonic white gaze, "'seeing' and attributing are indissoluble; they are part and parcel of the discursive power to name reality, which . . . is linked to institutional and material power."[20] It is through this endemic knowing in advance that Black lives are systemically devalued amidst a formally color-blind legal system.[21] The assertion that Black Lives Matter is thus powerful and subversive precisely because it foregrounds the reality that should be against the background reality that currently is: in (white) America, Black lives matter less.[22]

The ways in which Black lives are devalued are usefully illuminated by Foucault's discussion of what he termed "racist killing." In his *Society Must Be Defended* lectures, Foucault argued that "racism . . . is the precondition for exercising the right to kill."[23] Foucault used the term "racism" in a stylized way, using the "ism" in a manner similar to the ism in nationalism, that is, an ideology centered around putting the race first. The import of his statement is that for death to be inflicted on someone with societal imprimatur—out of a "right to kill"—the only justification in modern society would have to be racist, i.e., that the killing was necessary for protection of the race. Foucault clarifies that "killing" includes "every form of indirect murder: the fact of exposing someone to death, increasing the risk of death for some people, or, quite simply, political death, expulsion, rejection, and so on."[24]

When the brand of race works as intended, people can preconsciously race one another to determine whether someone is to be treated as a person simpliciter or as a subordinate person. When someone's racial designation is ambiguous, the background tool is foregrounded, and the process of racing becomes a conscious activity. A white person will be able to move freely within a (white) world that will afford them the rights and privileges owed to someone who is intrinsically valuable as an end in itself. A nonwhite person, however, particularly a Black person, will move through the (white) world always preceded by a brand that designates them as a subordinate person excluded from full membership in the rights and privileges of personhood. But the brand of race is not only a tool to exclude the branded from full participation in personhood; the brand also serves to designate the branded themselves as tools, beings with a structure of in-order-to-serve. Branded persons cannot move freely within a world by and for the unbranded and are instead confined to certain permissible ways of being in service to that world. When branded persons perform the supporting roles permitted to them, i.e., when branded persons know their place and stay in it, they become largely invisible as tools that recede into the background of the (white) world. But if branded persons move beyond the confines of the supporting roles permitted them, they become conspicuous as unruly elements that need to be put back in their place.[25]

Below I explore the phenomenology of the ontological subordination operant in race as it exists in contemporary (white) America. Drawing on the work of Africana phenomenologists, I argue that the experience of blackness involves an existential cleaving of the body from self through the ontological violence wrought upon the Black person by the (white) world.[26] As the Black person moves through the (white) world encumbered by a body branded with blackness, the (white) world primarily interacts with the Black person qua Black, not qua person, and the Black person is thus constantly forced to see themselves seen as less than one is on the basis of their marked body. The Black person's body is thus ripped from the invisible background of their everyday experience of self and thrust into the foreground as something obtrusive. By contrast, the experience of whiteness, by and large, involves a cohesive, embodied personhood. The white person moves through the (white) world unencumbered by a racial brand and thus never has to see themselves seen as a member of a subordinate category of being on the basis of their marked body. The white person's body instead recedes into the invisible background of everyday experience as they freely move about a world made by and for persons.

BLACKNESS AND ONTOLOGICAL SUBORDINATION

To live in the United States is to live in a world always already occupied by whiteness. To be a Black person living in the United States is to live in occupied territory. This occupation has important rules. As a Black person, to know the rules and follow them, to know that your place in (white) America is in service to whiteness, and to stay in your place is to have a chance at being left to fade into the inconspicuous background of the (white) American story. If you do not follow the rules of (white) America or challenge your place within it, however, you become conspicuous as a tool failing to perform its function, you are obtrusive as unruly and threatening to the order of things, and you court the violently corrective white gaze.

(White) America is a world that has been made by and for white persons. This world privileges whiteness through our laws as well as our individual and collective actions. White persons, unbranded by race, are able to move freely in this world. But persons branded by race, particularly those branded with blackness, move through this (white) world encumbered by their brand. This brand is ontological—it determines ways of being allowed to be in the (white) world—and results in a distinctly branded way of being in that world. Blackness implies a Black way of being in the (white) world. As a result, by necessity, persons branded with blackness develop distinct tools and know-how to move about the (white) world. These tools and know-how are necessary as a response to the ontological oppression implied by the brand of blackness, but they also constitute a basis for a distinct, rich, and complex Black world.[27] It is important to distinguish here between brandedness and identity; whereas brandedness is imposed through ontological power, identity is cocreated by and between persons in a shared world.[28]

The experience of blackness entails being subject to a world in which the Black person, qua person, is not seen, and the Black person sees themselves seen as something subordinate, reduced to roles supporting the (white) world. This is a world in which the Black person is invisible so long as they remain within the being in the world permitted them but in which they become hypervisible if they move beyond those boundaries. In turn, hypervisibility invites the punishing gaze of white supremacy.

Ralph Ellison's *Invisible Man* opens with the following lines:

> I am an invisible man . . . . I am invisible, understand, simply because people refuse to see me. Like the bodiless heads you see sometimes in circus sideshows, it is as though I have been surrounded by mirrors of hard, distorting glass. When they approach me they see only my surroundings, themselves, or figments of their imagination—indeed, everything and anything except me. Nor is my invisibility exactly a matter of a biochemical accident to my epidermis. That invisibility to which I refer occurs because of a peculiar disposition of the eyes of those with whom I come in contact. A matter of the construction of their inner eyes, those eyes with which they look through their physical eyes upon reality.[29]

These lines describe the experience of ontological brandedness. But understanding race as ontological brand reveals that the deficiency of the inner eye to which Ellison refers is not a deficiency at all; the invisibility is instead proof that the inner eye and the world it looks out upon work perfectly well: the eye is blind to the things that are as they should be.[30]

Because ontological branding results in visible identities,[31] seeing is a foundational activity in ontological oppression through brandedness.[32] As Yancy puts it, "the process of 'looking' . . . is a powerful act of construction" by which a person with certain phenotypic characteristics "is *ontologized* into" a *Black* person, and this "becoming" is "an act of dehumanization."[33] Note that the seeing is not the branding. The seeing results in ontologizing only because it participates in the practices of a world within which persons with these characteristics have always already been branded as black.[34] To return to the cattle brand example, we can say that the system of property protection through brands is maintained through the process of seeing—if the world went blind, the brands would cease to function—but it is not, of course, the seeing that brands. Instead, the seeing simply responds to the meaning given to the branding, a meaning derived from a work-world, the existence of which precedes the looking. But "[w]ithin this context, 'seeing' is not merely a private and isolated performance but the repetition of a collective performative gazing, the reproduction of the weight of a racist oracular epistemic order sustained by 'a culturally and structurally racist society.'"[35]

The branded are keenly aware of their brands, i.e., their attributed ontological inferiority, and are thus condemned to a conflicted identity, to a tension between the self as known and self as seen.[36] Compare the experience of W.E.B. Du Bois to George Yancy's a century later. Du Bois wrote that as a child "it dawned upon me with a certain suddenness that I was different from the others," and as an adult came to understand that segregationists had a "belief that Black folk are subhuman," where this belief arose out of a "passionate, deep seated heritage, and as such can be moved by neither argument nor fact."[37] For his part, Yancy describes the experience of car doors locking as he approaches: "the clicking sounds mark me; they inscribe me, materializing my presence, as it were, in ways that I know to be untrue. . . . As I endure those clicking sounds, I catch a glimpse of myself through the white person's gaze. I am constructed as evil and darkness. Like the night, I am to be avoided. After all, peril lurks in the dark." [38]

The Black person interacts with a (white) world that interacts with the Black person qua Black, not qua person. The Black person, qua person, is thus rendered invisible to the (white) world. This invisibility of the person is not the invisibility of tools. The invisibility of the person described here concerns depersonalization resulting in an imposed invisibility of personhood, which constitutes a form of ontological violence.[39] This depersonalization and rendering invisible of the Black person qua person involves, at least in part, an asymmetrical "*individualizing* White negativity and *generalizing* Black negativity."[40]

As an illustration, consider Bob, a Black man. Bob is Bob. Bob is who he is. He knows that. His family knows that. But when he is out in the (white) world, he senses that the world largely does not see him as Bob but as black-man$_{Bob}$.[41] His blackness precedes him.[42] And this brand of blackness marks him, creating a cleavage between himself and his marked body.[43] This creates a dualism the unbranded generally do not have to face. When a white man goes through the world, when a white man introduces himself, the world generally sees him as a person: "Oh, here is Sam doing this thing/wanting this thing/being this thing." And if Sam robs a liquor store for money to buy heroin, then the world will say Sam was sick, or Sam made some terrible choices. But if Bob robs a liquor store for money to buy heroin, the world will not say, "Bob has problems, let's pray for him." The world will say: "Alas. Black folks."[44] As Yancy puts it, whereas white persons have problems, Black persons *are* problems.[45]

Ontological brandedness allows the unbranded the experience of their personhood while cleaving the branded from themselves by imposing a distinction between themselves and their bodies. Racial domination works through brands that live on the body and become invisible to the unbranded where the phenomenological outcome is that brandedness becomes invisible to the unbranded while always remaining visible to the branded. This results in the imposed dualism experienced by the branded. Whereas as a white person, I would move about the (white) world as a person, seeing and being seen as a person, the experience would be very different if I were branded with blackness. As a Black person, I would move about the world with people seeing my brand, i.e., my marked body, making determinations on the basis of this marked body, even ascribing an identity on the basis of the marked body—all of which separates me from myself.[46]

This is something that white people do not experience vis-à-vis their racial designation, and men do not experience vis-à-vis their gender. No one really talks about male or white bodies because there are no male bodies, there are just men,[47] and there are no white bodies, there are just people.[48] As Ahmed explains,

> To be comfortable is to be so at ease with one's environment that it is hard to distinguish where one's body ends and the world begins. One fits. And in the act of fitting, the surfaces of bodies disappear from view. White bodies are comfortable as they inhabit spaces that extend their shape. The bodies and spaces "point" toward each other, as a "point" that is not seen as it is also "the point" from which we see.[49]

The unbranded can go through the world unaware that they are unbranded. That is the phenomenological lightness of unbrandedness, the unencumbered way of being allowed to be in the world. This is part of the spoils of privilege. The privilege is that you don't even know that you don't know that you don't know, and you don't even need to know for your purposes, because you experience a world oriented around you simply as "the way things are".[50]

It is different for the branded. "Bodies stand out when they are out of place," as Ahmed has noted, and the branded are very aware of their brand.[51] It is, in Coates' words, "the great barrier between the world and me."[52] The branded are reminded of it on a daily basis, and the personal cost this entails is part of the subordination of brandedness.[53] Race is experienced as a brand only for the branded, and the branded navigate between worlds where the brand differs in meaning, e.g., family, friends, close communities, and the Black world as opposed to the (white) world.[54]

The phenomenological result of ontological privilege is a cohesive experience of an embodied self, while the cost of branding is a dualism imposed by cleaving the body from the self, the inescapable and irreconcilable experience of myself being inside a body moving through space and time.⁵⁵ The branded person is, as Yancy describes, "forced into a state of doubleness, *seeing* himself as other"⁵⁶ through what Mills described as the "phenomenological experience of the disjuncture between official (white) reality and actual (nonwhite) experience, the 'double-consciousness' of which W.E.B. Du Bois spoke."⁵⁷ "For the black man," explains Ahmed, citing Frantz Fanon, "consciousness of the body is 'third person consciousness' and the feeling is one of negation."⁵⁸ The result, in Coates' words, is that a Black man's life becomes "a war for the possession of his body."⁵⁹ This state of being at war simply by virtue of being Black in (white) America is a continuation of the same ontological subordination that began in the times of slavery. The ability to have a cohesive identity is made difficult because the body is stolen. Appropriated. As Warren notes, "to be free is much more than a legal status (although it is often reduced to this); it is an onto-existential condition in which the human can engage in its primordial relation,"⁶⁰ and the steady march of freedom and equality that (white) America touts has left the fetters on Black being largely intact.

The branded experience their brandedness, particularly in the presence of the unbranded. Ordinary interactions with the unbranded provide constant reminders that the branded are branded, and they are seen through their brand. For the person of color, Yancy explains, moving through the (white) world "is like entering into a strange house that has acquired the shape of those who inhabit it, a space that speaks to their modes of traversing it."⁶¹ For persons of color, persons preceded by their branded bodies, moving through these spaces entails the encumbrance of constantly having one's body bumping up against things, the things placed there by and for somebody else's world. As David Polizzi notes, "black-being-in-the-world is figured by a social reality that defines blackness . . . as inferior and dangerous."⁶² For white persons, however, the experience is different because, as Yancy notes, "their white bodies can move with ease, unraced, comfortable, and safe."⁶³

Considering an elevator to explore this phenomenon, Yancy compares the difference between being in an elevator alone and being in an elevator with a white woman. When alone, Yancy writes,

> I have moved my body within the space of the elevator in a noncalculating fashion, paying no particular attention to my bodily comportment, the movement of my hands, my eyes, the position of my feet. I did not calculate the distance between my arm, hand, and my fingers in relationship to the buttons indicating the various floors. On such occasions, my "being-in" the space of the elevator is familiar; my bodily movements, my stance, are indicative of what it means to inhabit a space of familiarity. In short, it is a space within which I am meaningfully absorbed in the habitual everydayness of riding elevators.⁶⁴

By contrast, when Yancy finds himself in an elevator with a white woman,

> The apparent racial neutrality of the space within the elevator (when I am standing alone) has become . . . one filled with white normativity. . . . I no longer feel bodily expansiveness within the elevator, but corporeally constrained, limited. I now begin to calculate, paying almost neurotic attention to my body movements, making sure that this "Black object," what now feels like an appendage, a weight, is not too close, not too tall, not too threatening. . . . My lived-body comes back to me . . . as something to be dealt with, as a challenge. The gaze of the woman disrupts my habituated bodily comportment and I am thrown into an uncomfortable awareness of my body. Where I am standing, the color of my skin and my posture are, in a moment, foregrounded and I am suddenly aware of how I am being perceived.[65]

The joint gender-race dynamic in this anecdote cannot be dismissed, of course, and Yancy's Black-maleness is a presence in that elevator such that it is impossible to isolate the effect of blackness from the effect of maleness on the white woman. But for purposes of our analysis, Yancy's experience illustrates the difference between the cohesive unity of embodied personhood within a familiar space versus the third person consciousness of a self alienated from his own body. Of course, given the ontological mechanics of gender, the white woman, qua woman, may well have found herself similarly disembodied when she found herself in an elevator with a man.

Yancy is simultaneously invisible (Yancy notes how "the woman on the elevator [clutching her purse] does not really 'see' me")[66] and hypervisible (Yancy notes that Black persons are "stressed and their appearance becomes hypermarked against the unmarked spaces of white intelligibility").[67] This seeming paradox illustrates the distinction between the invisibility of the person and the invisibility of the tool. Yancy, a Black person, is invisible qua person because the woman on the elevator sees him qua Black, not qua person. But because Yancy, qua Black, is an in-order-to-serve the interests of the (white) world, he becomes hypervisible qua Black because unfamiliar Black men do not belong alone with white women. Yancy's hypervisibility is the obtrusiveness of a tool out of place. Yancy, qua Black, could perhaps have belonged, for example, as a janitor, and if Yancy had interacted with the elevator woman as her office building's friendly janitor, she may well have never clutched her purse because he would have been invisible both qua person and qua Black.

This is the phenomenon of Black invisibility and hypervisibility before the white gaze. The Black person who is what they are supposed to be and does what they are supposed to do is invisible. This is the invisibility of an inconspicuous tool performing as it should, but it is also the invisibility of a person unseen behind a brand they cannot remove. On the other hand, the

Black person who is not what they are supposed to be or not doing what they are supposed to be doing becomes hypervisible. This is the obtrusiveness of a tool malfunctioning or out of place. At the same time, however, the person as such remains unseen behind their brand. The hypervisibility is focused on an in-order-to-serve the interests of the (white) world failing to perform its function.

In interaction with a world by and for the unbranded, brandedness means a constant pressure to conform to the expectations attached to one's brand.[68] If I do so, if I behave within the confines of what is expected of me, I minimize my obtrusiveness within that world.[69] As regards race, it is as if my brand were a servant uniform designating me to a particular type of work for a lifetime, and sometimes I can even forget that I have it on. This is the conflicted and tortured comfort of invisibility Ellison describes:

> It is sometimes advantageous to be unseen, although it is most often rather wearing on the nerves. Then too, you're constantly being bumped against by those of poor vision. Or again, you often doubt if you really exist. You wonder whether you aren't simply a phantom in other people's minds.[70]

When acting within the confines of what is permitted, the branded becomes invisible to the unbranded. The kindly Black mail carrier, the charismatic (but humble) Black athlete, and the pious Black elder all fade into the background of everydayness as they play supporting roles to white protagonists living out their own stories. But if any of them get uppity or unruly—if the mail carrier strikes, if the athlete takes a knee, if the elder speaks of white supremacy—they become obtrusive, standing out like a servant greedily helping himself to the buffet he is supposed to be serving, and they court the attention of the white supremacist gaze that will seek to put them back in their place.[71]

Race makes (white) America a world normal for the unbranded, a world with which white people can be familiar and in which myriad social tools become invisible as (white) persons go about being in that world. But by the same token, race makes the (white) world unfamiliar per se to the branded; race guarantees that the branded will never be wholly at home in (white) America.[72] The experience of blackness in a white space is such that "within such spaces, one is hyperattentive to one's movements, to one's presence, and collective absence."[73] This places the Black person in an existential double bind. If I make peace with my brandedness, if I accept my place, if I behave that way, no boat will be rocked thereby, and I may be left alone or even rewarded. But that is not me. And if I want something else, something different, if I want my life to matter as much as everyone else's, now I'm wearing a servant uniform and wanting to sit down at the master's table.[74] As soon as I challenge the confines of my brand, my invisibility becomes hypervisibility.

I have, in Heidegger's words, "a heightened 'there.'"[75] I am obtrusive and invite the policing of the boundaries I transgressed.[76]

Challenging the confines of brandedness is fraught with peril. As Ellis writes, "[m]ost of the time . . . I remember that I am invisible and walk softly so as not to awaken the sleeping ones. Sometimes it is best not to awaken them; there are few things in the world as dangerous as sleepwalkers."[77] Kate Manne's analysis of misogyny is particularly useful in this regard. Manne argues that "misogyny should be understood as the 'law enforcement branch' of a patriarchal order, which has the overall function of *policing* and *enforcing* its governing norms and expectations."[78] Manne illuminates the dynamic of ontological oppression in a feminist context, where the boundaries between unbrandedness and brandedness—between manhood and womanhood—are enforced "by visiting hostile or adverse social consequences" on women who "violate or challenge the relevant norms or expectations."[79]

Manne elegantly captures the mechanics of subordination through ontological branding in her analysis of misogyny as

> primarily a property of social environments in which women are liable to encounter hostility due to the enforcement and policing of patriarchal norms and expectations—often, though not exclusively, insofar as they violate patriarchal law and order. Misogyny hence functions to enforce and police women's subordination and to uphold male dominance, against the backdrop of other intersecting systems of oppression and vulnerability, dominance and disadvantage, as well as disparate material resources, enabling and constraining social structures, institutions, bureaucratic mechanisms, and so on.[80]

White supremacy similarly threatens persons of color with hostile consequences if they challenge their status as ontologically subordinate.[81] This racial oppression plays out as part of a larger system of policing and enforcing the boundaries between ontological brandedness and unbrandedness.[82] The race problem in America is, thus, ultimately not about racial difference but about the subordination of persons of color for the sake of maintaining white supremacy.[83] The dramatic legal changes that have transpired since slavery have left the underlying ontology intact. As Warren explains, the transformation of the Black person from chattel to equal citizen is illusory because it "is really just a move from the particular (single master) to the universal (community of whites/Mitsein), a transformation that retains slavery in essence."[84]

Brandedness presents the branded with an impossible existential choice: sacrifice your authenticity or sacrifice what little safety you have in the (white) world.[85] This is a fundamental difference in experience between the branded and the unbranded.[86] The unbranded never experience a situation in which they are acting beyond the confines of the position permitted to their racial group. For the branded, however, such experiences come early and often as they are acutely aware of the restricted sphere to which they are expected to limit themselves. The reality is that, as Polizzi writes, "flight from racial oppression in America is impossible."[87] This presents a constant and unavoidable existential question—as Coates puts it: "how do I live free in this black body?"[88]

One answer lies in the creation of a Black world. A world by and for the branded is defined by the distinct toolset and know-how needed to navigate as branded through the world of the unbranded.[89] Yancy observes that "Black people constitute a kind of 'epistemological community' (a community of knowers)," where membership in this community is mediated through the shared "background histories of oppression that Blacks have experienced vis-à-vis whites."[90] This epistemic community shares a toolset, a know-how for maneuvering through the (white) world while encumbered by the brand of race.[91] This knowhow "speaks to a socially and behaviorally complex way in which Black persons have had to organize the world and recognize how that world is organized in ways that systemically and systematically vitiate their dignity and literally reduce them to a state of nonbeing."[92] To be a member of this community of shared know-how, to be at home in this *world*, is to "understand one's relationship to a historical community" through a dance between one's "objective social location" and the "negotiation of the meaning and implications of one's identity."[93]

The Black world is beautifully described by Coates:

> I knew that I wasn't so much bound to a biological "race" as to a group of people, and these people were not black because of any uniform color or any uniform physical feature. They were bound because they suffered under the weight of the [White Supremacist] Dream, and they were bound by all the beautiful things, all the language and mannerisms, all the food and music, all the literature and philosophy, all the common language that they fashioned like diamonds under the weight of the Dream. . . . In other words, I was part of a world.[94]

The blackness described here is not the blackness of imposed inferiority determined by the (white) world. This blackness is instead an embodied identity collectively forged in resistance to oppression.[95] The Black world was in turn "forged in the shadow of the murdered, the raped, the disembodied," and yet, of utmost importance—particularly considering the centuries of ontological violence waged on blackness—Coates declares that this world, this home, is "as beautiful as any other."[96] "They made us into a race," Coates declares. "We made ourselves into a people."[97]

But it is here that we see one of the most insidious dimensions of ontological oppression: ontological brands operate even within branded communities.[98] The branded, too, have been learning and growing in this (white) world, and the branded have also learned to race and act accordingly.[99] The branded are seen as subordinate, and unbrandedness is privileged even through the eyes of the branded. This is why implicit bias is not just a white phenomenon.[100] This is why the critique of racism in police brutality is not rebutted by pointing to Black police officers committing offenses. This is the cruelest of all results. Because I am always already in this (white) world, race unavoidably provides a "necessary background from which I know myself."[101] I cannot unsee the brand of race even in myself, and when I look in the mirror the brand stands even between myself and me.[102] In this (white) world, as Coates puts it, "it is difficult for Blacks to be 'just me.'"[103]

But the Black world is not safe. The Black world always exists against a (white) America that regards the Black world through the same instrumental value it ascribes to blackness generally. The Black world, at best, is a rich source of culture and resources. (White) America is enamored with the contributions that blackness has made to music, art, and fashion, even as Black persons are routinely excluded from the spoils that flow from the commercialization of these resources. The Black world, in other words, becomes another site to colonize and exploit what Coates calls plunder.[104] But if the Black world moves beyond a state of benign cultural resource and begins to assert its integrity and autonomy, it becomes obtrusive and dangerous. Discussing the ways in which (white) America perceived Malcolm X and Black nationalism, Polizzi notes that "blacks defending themselves against personal attack fell outside the limits of what the racist they-self could allow Black-being-in-the-world and, therefore, viewed this possibility as a deliberate and serious threat to its authority."[105]

WHITENESS AND ONTOLOGICAL PRIVILEGE

(White) America is a world that has been made by and for white persons.[106] This world privileges whiteness through our laws as well as our collective and individual actions. White persons, unbranded by race, can move freely in this world, enjoying the ontological privilege of unencumbered access to ways of being in the world. In (white) America, the "objective" world is white, and it is filled with "white spaces," i.e., "spaces of familiarity that are already given before the moment of an individual white person's arrival."[107] Ultimately, white persons get to be at home in a world oriented around whiteness.[108] To dwell in this white world as a white person is to deploy a particular toolset and know-how, where the know-how includes mastery of the art of racing, i.e., mastery in the art of seeing a person's ontological brandedness and acting accordingly.[109] Whiteness is, as Yancy puts it, an "act of performance sustained and justified by individual and institutional practices."[110]

Part of the spoils (and/or cost) of ontological privilege is blindness to that very privilege.[111] It is difficult to see your lack of distance from the norm. Just like we are blind to our standing at an appropriate distance from someone when we speak with them, the unbranded are generally blind to the ontological oppression of the branded and their own being privileged thereby. As Ahmed explains,

> [w]hite bodies do not have to face their whiteness; they are not oriented 'toward' it.... By not having to encounter being white as an obstacle, given that whiteness is 'in line' with what is already given, bodies that pass as white move easily, and this motility is extended by what they move toward.[112]

As Yancy puts it, quoting Sullivan, "whiteness is a powerful embodied form of being-in-the-world, where 'ignorance of white domination is not just an empty gap in knowledge nor the product of a mere epistemological oversight.'"[113] The upshot is that in (white) America, "the socially constructed allure, power, and hegemony of whiteness are passed off as the 'natural' order of things."[114]

Ontological branding has created blackness and rendered those branded with blackness as ontologically subordinate entities properly relegated to roles in service of the (white) world. In this manner, historically and daily, naturally and invisibly, (white) America understands Black lives to matter less than white lives. When a white child is killed by a gun, we grieve them, often nationally. Think of the child—we hear—the family, the community. When Black children are killed by guns, however, well, it is sad—the background narrative goes—but, you know, it's just not the same. Their lives were not the same. Their environment. Everything that is different about them and everything that is wrong with the circumstances that led to the violence that killed them can be traced back to the simple fact that they are in a different (read: inferior) place, and it would be wrong to expect from them what we expect from normal (read: white, read: superior) America.[115]

Especially in today's political climate, white privilege has become a flashpoint. Many poor and middle-class white persons bitterly resent the suggestion that they enjoy a privileged existence, as if the color of their skin made fortunes rain down on them like manna from heaven. There has been a steady rise of reverse-racism claims in recent years, as well as an increase in claims of Black privilege. But white privilege and white supremacy are not inoculations against a difficult life. A white person may be ontologically privileged in the racial dimension and still be subordinated, exploited, or marginalized in other contexts.[116] White privilege has thus proven notoriously difficult to articulate, in particular, to this sector, the sector that, perhaps—especially if one subscribes to the understanding that the interests of working-class persons are significantly aligned, regardless of race—is most in need of understanding the claim. It is thus imperative that white privilege be understood in the right frame. Understanding white privilege as ontological disparity may help advance the conversation without being subject to needless misunderstandings or accusations.

As Zack notes, white privilege is manifest in tangible rights granted to white persons:

> Often (but not always), what is called a "white privilege" that nonwhites lack, is a right that is protected for whites and not for nonwhites. That is, a "privilege" whites are said to have is sometimes a right belonging to both whites and nonwhites that is violated when nonwhites are the ones who own it.[117]

These rights include property rights, due process rights, and the right to self-defense. But white privilege is also existential; it is the privilege to be presumptively at home in (white) America. The privilege of whiteness is a way of being in the world, an ontological openness that comes from being in one's own home such that all things and spaces are (supposed to be) available for your use and enjoyment.[118] As heirs of the colonialism-Enlightenment project, persons privileged by whiteness get to move through (white) America with a sense of entitlement to space and resources without questioning their commitment to universal human equality.

The upshot is that within the framework of (white) American values, the unbranded are likely to believe that successes and failures are generally attributable to themselves.[119] From the vantage of whiteness, I see a system that, while imperfect, generally speaking, gives everyone willing to work hard and take personal responsibility a fair shake. Victims of society are thus people that make excuses because if I were to end up in the position of one of those so-called social victims, I know that it would be because of my failings, not society's. By extension, the current racial disparities seen in social, economic, political, and cultural power in the United States can be understood as the effects of poor collective choices by individuals who are not where they would like to be. This is the logic at play in the *Parents Involved* Supreme Court decision, what Mills calls "an epistemology of ignorance."[120]

Consider the simple example of how one, viz., a white person, routinely breaks the law in the ordinary course of everyday life. Speeding. Jaywalking. Recreational drugs. The experience of these legal breaches, if they rise to conscious consideration at all, is one of simple cost-benefit analysis. By contrast, a person of color, especially a Black person, traverses the everydayness of (white) American life facing the reality that any legal infraction carries with it the possibility of violence or death.[121] To live everyday life the way one does in America is something available to white persons and denied to persons of color, especially Black persons.

White privilege entails the ontological subordination of persons of color, rendering them only conditionally American, subject to their comportment in accordance with their permitted ways of being in the world. Consider the right to self-defense vis-à-vis the government in this light. (White) America touts slogans such as "Give me liberty or give me death!" or "Live free or die!" Within the (white) American narrative, the soul of the Constitution is embodied in We the People, not in the government as such. For this reason, it can be patriotic to take anti-government action. But this is not the case for Black Americans, who are instead expected to show their patriotism by not rocking the boat, by staying in their place.[122]

When race operates as it is supposed to, when everyone is fulfilling their proper roles, when the tool of race recedes into the invisibility of familiarity, from the vantage point of whiteness, race itself seems to vanish. But, as Mills notes, "the only people who can find it psychologically possible to deny the centrality of race are those who are racially privileged, for whom race is invisible precisely because the world is structured around them, whiteness as the ground against which the figures of other races—those who, unlike us, are raced—appear."[123] The unbranded are born into a world that has always already been populated by branded and unbranded persons, and because the experience of the unbranded within that world is one of familiarity, the branded have no reason to see race as anything other than ontic reality.

Whiteness is hegemonic and invisible, universal as the norm and particular as the persons wielding its privilege. As Taylor explains,

> [i]n the face of the work of racializing other bodies and thereby subjecting them to violence, whiteness does the strangest thing, it disappears. Rather than boldly identifying itself as master and supreme, whiteness makes a calculated move to always hide itself behind the gaze of normality. This is as true now as it was in the age of Bernier and Kant. Whiteness disappears, and the greatest threat and the supreme danger of whiteness comes to the fore when whiteness no longer shows itself.[124]

When persons of color act beyond the boundaries permitted them—i.e., when persons of color act as if they enjoyed the same rights as white persons—white privilege is threatened, and many white persons experience this as an existential threat, the experience of a world being lost,[125] what Warren terms ontological terror.[126] We then enter the realm where (white) America feels threatened because the ontological boundaries upon which (white) America has been constructed are under threat. In Ahmed's words, "when bodies arrive that seem 'out of place,' [e.g., a Black man in the White House], it involves disorientation: people blink and then look again. The proximity of such bodies makes familiar spaces seem strange. 'People are thrown because a whole worldview is jolted.'"[127] It is perhaps not surprising that this existential threat is experienced acutely by so-called working-class white persons, persons for whom ontological privilege may be experienced as particularly important.[128] And it is perhaps not surprising that the reaction to such ontological boundary transgression should be so passionate, or even violent. In Coates' words, "[h]ate gives identity. The nigger, the fag, the bitch illuminate the border, illuminate what we ostensibly are not, illuminate the Dream of being white, of being a Man. We name the hated strangers and are thus confirmed in the tribe."[129]

NOTES

1. Yancy, *Black Bodies, White Gazes*, 69.

2. Yancy, *Black Bodies, White Gazes*, 84; see Peller, *Critical Race Consciousness*, 149 ("the most successful form of social power is one that presents itself not as power, but as reason, truth, and objectivity").

3. Sally Haslanger, "Tracing the Sociopolitical Reality of Race," in *What is Race* (Cambridge: Oxford University Press, 2019), 29 (describing racial identity as a "kind of know-how for navigating one's position in radicalized social space").

4. Cf Foucault, *Society Must Be Defended*, 38–39 (discussing "codes of normalization" and "normalizing society").

5. Yancy, *Black Bodies, White Gazes*, 64 (describing a child's racism: "the young white boy dwells within/ experiences/ engages the world of white racist practices in such a way that the practices qua racist practices have become invisible. The young boy's response is part and parcel of an implicit knowledge of how he gets around in a Manichean world. Being-in a racist world, a lived context of historicity, the young boy does not "see" the dark body as "dark" and then thematically proceed to apply negative value predicates to it,... the young white boy is situated within a familiar white racist world of intelligibility, one that has already "accepted" whiteness as "superior" and Blackness as "inferior" and "savage."... His white racist performance is a form of everyday coping within the larger unthematized world of white social coping. The socio-ontological structure that gives intelligibility to the young white boy's racist performance is prior to a set of beliefs of which he is reflectively aware.").

6. Alcoff, *Visible Identities*, 185 ("Racial knowledges exist at the site of common sense.").

7. Mills, *Racial Contract*, 95; Taylor, *Techno-Racism*, 45.

8. Yancy, *Black Bodies, White Gazes*, 224 (noting that "transacting with flesh and blood bodies of color can function as a powerful catalyst that can trigger an ambush" against whiteness).

9. Yancy, *Black Bodies, White Gazes*, 133; Alcoff, *Phenomenology of Racial Embodiment* 184.

10. In Heidegger's words, something unfamiliar "stands in the way, comes at an inconvenient time, is uncomfortable, disturbing, awkward, hindering. As such, it has... a heightened 'there.'" Heidegger, *Ontology*, 77.

11. Heidegger, *Ontology*, 72.

12. Cf Ahmed, *Queer Phenomenology*, 141 (discussing the in-principle neutral phenomenon of how the stranger is part of the familiar world, that the stranger is already "at home" and is familiar in its "strangeness.")

13. Consider Yancy's observation that "Black people constitute a kind of 'epistemological community' (a community of knowers)." Yancy, *Black Bodies, White Gazes*, 23. See Peller, *Critical Race Consciousness*, 37 (discussing the difference between white "ethnic heritage" and the racial identity of an oppressed group). Compare with Foucault's discussion of "subjugated knowledge." Foucault, *Society Must Be Defended*, 7. Cf. Manne, *Down Girl*, 66 (prejudice against women would be an "individual quirk or something like a phobia absent a system of patriarchal oppression in the background."); Peller, *Critical Race Consciousness*, 34–35 (discussing the Black nationalist critique of a "neutral theory of knowledge").

14. The mechanics of ontological branding are helpfully revealed through this phenomenon of the "exotic." As Yancy argues through a thought experiment, imagine that the *Plessy v. Ferguson* case is being televised, and imagine a viewer who knows that Plessy is 1/8 Black. Although Plessy "looked white" to just about anyone, this knowledge of what he "really" is informs the viewer's cognition such that "despite his phenotypic whiteness, [the viewer] would come to react to him in ways that she would react to [a] black body.... [H]er physical eyes may see white skin, but her gaze eventually overrides what is visual." Yancy, *Black Bodies, White Gazes*, 31. Cf. Mills, *Black Rights/White Wrongs*, 123; Manne, *Down Girl*, 66 (prejudice against women would be an "individual quirk or something like a phobia absent a system of patriarchal oppression in the background.").

15. Consider, for example, the experience of one of Yancy's Black students, who, "when a white academic counselor at one university, after the student disclosed that he received a scholarship, asked him, 'So, which sport do you play?'" Yancy, *Black Bodies, White Gazes*, 28. Cf. Peller, *Critical Race Consciousness*, 13 (discussing how the "residue" of "the subordination of African Americans was rationalized, legalized, and (more generally) normalized" in a post-*Brown* South.); Ahmed, *Queer Phenomenology*, 132–133.

16. E.g., Keith Payne et al., "How to Think about 'Implicit Bias,'" 30 *Scientific American* 3 (Summer 2021): 32; Mills, *Racial Contract*, 89.

17. Cf. Anne E. Cudd, *Analyzing Oppression* (Oxford: Oxford University Press, 2006), 85; Yancy, *Black Bodies, White Gazes*, 246 (quoting Levinas: "violence does not consist so much in injuring and annihilating persons as in interrupting their continuity, making them play roles in which they no longer recognize themselves, making them betray not only commitments but their own substance, making them carry out actions that will destroy every possibility for action.").

18. Yancy, *Black Bodies, White Gazes*, 17.

19. Yancy, *Black Bodies, White Gazes*, 6.

20. Yancy, *Black Bodies, White Gazes*, 6.

21. Haslanger, Sally, "Gender and race: (What) are they? (What) do we want them to be?," 34 *Noûs* 1 (2000): 31–55, 40 (discussing racial oppression in the "normal processes of everyday life").

22. Mills, *Racial Contract*, 85 (arguing that because white lives matter more, brown crimes against white lives are the most egregious); Zack, *White Privilege and Black Rights*, 29 ("What it credibly means to say that black lives do not matter in America is that compared to white lives, they are not treated with the same respect and concern and there are not comparable efforts taken to preserve and protect black lives.").

23. Foucault, *Society Must Be Defended*, 256.

24. Foucault, *Society Must Be Defended*, 256. Cf. Andrea Gawrylewski, "The Case for Antiracism" *Scientific American*, Summer 2021.

25. Sheth, *Toward a Political Philosophy of Race*.

26. E.g., Yancy, *Black Bodies, White Gazes*, 32 (describing that the lived-body begins to feel like something ontologically occurrent, something merely there in its facticity).

27. Coates, *Between the World and Me*, 42, 120; Yancy, *Black Bodies, White Gazes*, 112 (discussing Black being-in-the-world); Peller, *Critical Race Consciousness*, 100 ("African Americans and whites in general inhabit significantly—though, of course, not totally—different cultural spaces.").

28. See Linda, *Visible Identities*.

29. Ralph Ellison, *Invisible Man* (New York: Modern Library, 1994), 3.

30. Cf. Mills, *Black Rights/ White Wrongs*, 54 (discussing invisible man).

31. Cf. Martín Alcoff, *Visible Identities*.

32. Yancy, *Black Bodies, White Gazes*, 91 ("[T]he construction of the phantasmic object must involve a constant process of maintenance... to maintain ignorance regarding the role that one plays in the construction.").

33. Yancy, *Black Bodies, White Gazes*, 93.

34. Yancy, *Black Bodies, White Gazes*, 91.

35. Yancy, *Black Bodies, White Gazes*, 224.

36. Mills, *Black Rights/ White Wrongs*, 53 ("what people of color come to see—in a sense the primary epistemic principle of the racialized social epistemology of which they are the object—is that they are not seen at all.").

37. Du Bois, *Souls of Black Folk*, 4; Du Bois, *Darkwater: Voices from Within the Veil* (New York: Harcourt, Brace, and Howe, 1920), 39, 73; Polizzi, *A Phenomenological Hermeneutic*, 9.

38. Yancy, *Black Bodies, White Gazes*, xxxiii–xxxiv; Baldwin, *Not Your Negro*, 39 ("I'm terrified at the moral apathy, the death of the heart, which is happening in my country. These people have deluded themselves for so long that they really don't think I'm human. And I base this on their conduct, not on what they say. And this means that they have become in themselves moral monsters.").

39. Yancy, *Black Bodies, White Gazes*, 68 ("Felt invisibility is a form of ontological and epistemological violence.").

40. Kendi, *Stamped from the Beginning*, 43.

41. Given the complexities of the relationship between race and gender, between white and male privilege, it is worth exploring the possibility of "Black man" and

"Black woman" operating as distinct brands. Black men seem to present a particular threat to white manhood, and it is thus likely not the case that Black men simply enjoy an overall more privileged position than Black women by virtue of their male privilege.

42. Cf. Ahmed, *Queer Phenomenology*, 141 (discussing how, for white persons, the body "trails behind", whereas for persons of color, the body precedes you and "catches you out.").

43. Cf. Martín Alcoff, *Visible Identities*, 184.

44. Yancy, *Black Bodies, White Gazes*, 43.

45. Yancy, *Black Bodies, White Gazes*, 80, 120 (to be Black is to be "an ontological problem, in a white supremacist society, one predicated on white power and privilege"); Jacqueline Johnson, "Mass Incarceration: a Contemporary Mechanism of Racialization in the United States" 47 *Gonzaga Law Review* 301–318 (2012).

46. Yancy, *Black Bodies, White Gazes*, 105 ("The Black body, through the hegemony of the white gaze, undergoes a phenomenological return that leaves it distorted and fixed as an essence.").

47. Cf. MacKinnon, *Toward a Feminist Theory of the State*, 218, 243 (discussing that men are by definition "not different"); Mills, *Racial Contract*, 53.

48. Ahmed, *Queer Phenomenology*, 132. Consider the slogans of liberation: "my body, my choice"; "our minds, our bodies".

49. Ahmed, *Queer Phenomenology*, 134–135.

50. Mills, Racial Contract, 30.

51. Ahmed, *Queer Phenomenology*, 135.

52. Coates, *Between the World and Me*, 65.

53. With white-as-human, "blacks will be the race most alienated from their own bodies—a fate particularly painful for black women, who, like all women, will... be valued chiefly by their physical appearance" Mills, *Racial Contract*, 62.

54. Coates, *Between the World and Me*, 120 (in "the beauty of my black world," Coates can "feel myself disappear on the streets of Harlem"); Yancy, *Black Bodies, White Gazes*, 106 (the Black world is defined by Black know-how, which is itself inextricable from maneuvering as branded in a world by and for the unbranded).

55. Mills, *Racial Contract*, 51.

56. Yancy, *Black Bodies, White Gazes*, 79.

57. Mills, *Racial Contract*, 109; W.E.B. Du Bois, *The Souls of Black Folk* (New York: The Modern Library, 2003). See discussion of the One, *supra*.

58. Ahmed, *Queer Phenomenology*, 139.

59. Coates, *Between the World and Me*, 18, 44, 49 (discussing this phenomenon as "dispossession" and the "loss of my body"). Note also "disembodiment" as discussed by Coates, *Between the World and Me*, 114 ("Disembodiment is a kind of terrorism, and the threat of it alters the orbit of all our lives and, like terrorism, this distortion is intentional."). See Yancy, *Black Bodies, White Gazes*, 17 ("The Black body has been confiscated."); 19 ("From the context of my lived experience, I feel "external," as it were, to my body, delivered and sealed in white lies."); 57 (The white gaze "returned me to myself as something I did not recognize.").

60. Warren, *Ontological Terror*, 50.

61. Yancy, *Black Bodies White Gazes*, 9.
62. Polizzi, *A Phenomenological Hermeneutic*, 6.
63. Yancy, *Black Bodies White Gazes*, 9.
64. Yancy, *Black Bodies White Gazes*, 31.
65. Yancy, *Black Bodies White Gazes*, 32.
66. Yancy, *Black Bodies White Gazes*, 21.
67. Yancy, *Black Bodies White Gazes*, 9.
68. Mills, *Black Rights/ White Wrongs*, 68.
69. Cf. Kendi, *Stamped from the Beginning*, 219 (on Lincoln declaring that the Black race "could never be placed on an equality with the white race," and that Black folks should thus "[s]acrifice something of your present comfort," and leave for Liberia. It was not Black presence that was the problem; it was Black freedom).
70. Ellison, *Invisible Man*, 3.
71. Recall Coates' experience when his son was shoved. This experience underscores the danger of being "uppity," the danger in forgetting there is no right to self-defense. "I had forgotten the rules, an error as dangerous on the Upper West Side of Manhattan as on the Westside of Baltimore. One must be without error out here. Walk in single file. Work quietly. Pack an extra number 2 pencil. Make no mistakes." Coates, *Between the World and Me*, 95. See Yancy, *Black Bodies, White Gazes*, 10 (discussing constantly wondering whether you have truly mastered the rules of the white space). Unruliness and uppitiness are examples of the ontological encumbrance imposed on the branded. Enforcement through punishment—in an extreme form it is physical death (lynchings, extrajudicial killings)—but in a less extreme form it is engendering a resentment. Kendi, *Stamped from the Beginning*, 505 (The uppity, successful-despite-the-game-being-rigged-against-you Black folks are the ones most resented). Discussing lynching, McWhorter explains that the principal purpose of lynching was disciplinary and has evolved into the penal system we have today. McWhorter, *Racism and Sexual Oppression in Anglo-America*, 159 ("Lynching was intended to instill a crippling fear in every African American who might ever think of achieving something or of distinguishing him- or herself in any way. To stand out was to risk being picked off. The safest thing to do was to blend in, stay with the group, raise neither voices nor eyes, and never, ever assert oneself"), 161 (arguing that lynching has evolved into the carceral system); Alexander, *The New Jim Crow*; Sheth, *Toward a Political Philosophy of Race*.
72. Yancy, *Black Bodies, White Gazes*, 18.
73. Yancy, *Black Bodies, White Gazes*, 9. As Sara Ahmed puts it, "[if] the world is made white, then the body at home is one that can inhabit whiteness." Ahmed, *Queer Phenomenology*, 111.
74. Mills, *Black Rights/ White Wrongs*, 68; Yancy, *Black Bodies, White Gazes*, 67.
75. Heidegger, *Ontology*, 77.
76. Ahmed, *Queer Phenomenology*, 135 (discussing how one learns to fade into the background, but sometimes you cannot); Yancy, *Black Bodies, White Gazes*, 9.
77. Ellison, *Invisible Man*, 5.
78. Manne, *Down Girl*, 78 (emphasis in original); 13 ("Misogyny does this by visiting hostile or adverse social consequences on a certain (more or less circumscribed)

class of girls or women to enforce and police social norms that are gendered either in theory (i.e., content) or in practice (i.e., norm enforcement mechanisms).")
79. Manne, *Down Girl*, 13, 20.
80. Manne, *Down Girl*, 20.
81. Manne, *Down Girl*, 20; see Sheth, *Toward a Political Philosophy of Race*; McWhorter, *Racism and Sexual Oppression in Anglo-America*, 161.
82. Manne, *Down Girl*, 63.
83. Racial oppression is distinct but not separate from other kinds of ontological oppression: "to truly be antiracists, we must also oppose all of the sexism, homophobia, colorism, ethnocentrism, nativism, cultural prejudice, and class bias teeming and teaming with racism to harm so many Black lives." Kendi, *Stamped from the Beginning*, 502–503.
84. Warren, *Ontological Terror*, 93.
85. Polizzi, *A Phenomenological Hermeneutic*, 7 (addressing the constraints on Black being in the world); Coates, *Between the World and Me*, 117 (discussing not feeling at home in the white world). The ontological branding model sheds important light on the phenomenon of covering. See Kenji Yoshino, *Covering: The Hidden Assault on Our Civil Rights* (New York: Random House, 2006). Covering can be understood as the attempt to hide the brand, to reduce as much as possible the distance between the position my brandedness grants me and the state of unbrandedness. Ahmed, *Queer Phenomenology*, 175 (discussing how the possibility of "closeting" an identity is "an orientation device, a way of inhabiting the world or of being at home in the world."); Yancy, *Black Bodies, White Gazes*, 74; Mills, *Black Rights/ White Wrongs*, 53. Along with this, ontological branding results in a distinct culture of the branded within which camps form around various approaches for dealing with brandedness.
86. Cf. Yancy, *Black Bodies, White Gazes*, xxx; 58; Warren, *Ontological Terror*, 107; Ahmed, *Queer Phenomenology*, 133 ("Whiteness is only invisible for those who inhabit it, or for those who get so used to its inhabitance that they learn not to see it, even when they are not it.").
87. Polizzi, *A Phenomenological Hermeneutic*, 26.
88. Coates, *Between the World and Me*, 12.
89. Coates, *Between the World and Me*, 56 ("I knew that we were something, that we were a tribe—on the one hand, invented, and on the other, no less real.").
90. Yancy, *Black Bodies, White Gazes*, 23. Compare with Foucault's discussion of "subjugated knowledge." Foucault, *Society Must Be Defended*, 7.
91. Cf. Yancy, *Black Bodies, White Gazes*, 111–112.
92. See Yancy, *Black Bodies, White Gazes*, 23. Cf Peller, *Critical Race Consciousness*, 135 (arguing for a distinction between essence and existence as regards "blackness").
93. Yancy, *Black Bodies, White Gazes*, 112.
94. Coates, *Between the World and Me*, 119–120.
95. Cf. Yancy, *Black Bodies, White Gazes*, 113 ("Black embodied subjectivity" is about "creating ways of combating anti-Black racist effects, and making sense of what it means to be Black-in-the-world."); 113 ("Blackness is a lived existential project.").

96. Coates, *Between the World and Me*, 120–121.

97. Coates, *Between the World and Me*, 149; Polizzi, *A Phenomenological Hermeneutic*, 8, 116 (discussing the way in which a Black world is experienced as racist and a threat to (white) America). Cf. Ahmed, *Queer Phenomenology*, 114. For a discussion of the rejection of a notion of a Black world due to its threat to the narrative that undergirds American white supremacy see Peller, *Critical Race Consciousness*, 117 ("whites saw in Black life only the harmful consequences of racial hierarchy and simply never considered the possibility that African Americans had constructed a cultural community worth preserving").

98. Mills, *Racial Contract*, 89.

99. There is a process for learning how to see and be seen in a dehumanized manner. Mills, *Racial Contract*, 87–88; Yancy, *Black Bodies, White Gazes*, 94 (discussing the "psychological duress of seeing herself through the white symbols that ontologized her into the epitome of grotesqueness.").

100. Cf. Kendi, *Stamped from the Beginning*, 10.

101. Alcoff (towards a phenomenology of racial embodiment) quoted in Ahmed, *Queer Phenomenology*, 13.

102. Coates, *Between the World and Me*; Toni Morrison, *The Bluest Eye* (New York: Vintage Books, 1970); Richard Rodriguez, *Days of Obligation: An Argument with my Mexican Father* (New York: Penguin, 1992).

103. Yancy, *Black Bodies, White Gazes*, 67.

104. Coates, *Between the World and Me*, 20; Yancy, *Black Bodies, White Gazes*, 91 (discussing colonialism as an ongoing and the endless project).

105. Polizzi, *A Phenomenological Hermeneutic*, 133.

106. Cf Peller, *Critical Race Consciousness*, 61 (discussing the Civil Rights-era integrationist "den[ial] that the world to which the Black middle class aspired was racially identifiable as a particularly white world, rather than a realm of universal, culturally neutral social practices.").

107. Yancy, *Black Bodies, White Gazes*, 8–9. Cf. MacKinnon, *Toward a Feminist Theory of the State*, 221.

108. Ahmed, *Queer Phenomenology*, 138.

109. This white orientation toward the white world—something unavailable to persons branded as nonwhite—constitutes what Yancy calls "whitely-being-in-the-world." Yancy, *Black Bodies, White Gazes*, 19; 41 ("Acting whitely might be described as a form of orientation that... unconsciously or pre-reflectively positions the white self vis-à-vis the nonwhite self.").

110. Yancy, *Black Bodies, White Gazes*, 153.

111. Mills, *Black Rights/ White Wrongs*, 47, 51. On the "pay off" of whiteness, see Mills, *Black Rights/ White Wrongs*, 114; Peller, *Critical Race Consciousness*, 64 (discussing how Civil Rights-era "whites as a group never considered the possibility that race consciousness might have a liberating rather than repressive, meaning."); Polizzi, *A Phenomenological Hermeneutic*, 135; MacKinnon, *Toward a Feminist Theory of the State*, 240; Taylor, *Techno-Racism*, 27.

112. Ahmed, *Queer Phenomenology*, 132. Cf. Yancy, *Black Bodies, White Gazes*, 245 ("[W]hite embodiment has inherited a history that resides in and through the

white body, a white racist history that saturates white modes of being."); Yoshino, *Covering*, 72.

113. Yancy, *Black Bodies, White Gazes*, 220.

114. Yancy, *Black Bodies, White Gazes*, 206.

115. Mills, *Racial Contract*, 101 (discussing how white lives matter: "feelings of vastly different outrage over white and nonwhite death, white and nonwhite suffering.").

116. See Manne, *Down Girl*, 46.

117. Zack, *White Privilege and Black Rights*, 3–4.

118. Mills, *Black Rights/ White Wrongs*, 48 (arguing that "whiteness itself becomes "property," underwriting a set of baseline entitlements and "reasonable" expectations that are part of one's legitimate rights as full citizen."). See Peller, *Critical Race Consciousness*, 128; Taylor, *Techno-Racism*, 47.

119. Mills, *Black Rights/ White Wrongs*, 48; Mills, *Racial Contract*, 33–34.

120. Mills, *Racial Contract*, 93; Peller, "Privilege," 897.

121. Natapoff, *Punishment Without Crime*, 3, 7, 160.

122. Baldwin, *Not Your Negro* 81; Coates, *Between the World and Me*, 32; Peller, *Critical Race Consciousness*, 44.

123. Mills, *Racial Contract*, 76.

124. Taylor, *Techno-Racism*, 79; Yancy, *Black Bodies, White Gazes*, 219.

125. Wildman, Stephanie M. "The Persistence of White Privilege" 18 *Wash. U. J. L. & Pol'y* 245 (2005).

126. Warren, *Ontological Terror*, 53; Mills, *Racial Contract*, 82. Ontological privilege is not an unconditional good, however. Ontological privilege might imply power and existential spoils, but this is not necessarily a better or ultimately freeing state of being. The unbranded "too is a prisoner of her own historically inherited imaginary and the habitual racist performances that have become invisible to her." Yancy, *Black Bodies, White Gazes*, 36; 220 ("racism eats away, as W. E. B. Du Bois might say, at the souls of white folk").

127. Ahmed, *Queer Phenomenology*, 135. Consider the sentiments of many white Americans feeling like a strangers in their "own" land, or this being an America they do not recognize anymore.

128. Yancy, *Black Bodies, White Gazes*, 20 ("the poor white body is invested in its whiteness in ways that are precisely designed to offset the variable of poverty"); Kendi, *Stamped from the Beginning*, 504. See Manne, *Down Girl*, for an analogous discussion on gender.

129. Coates, *Between the World and Me*, 60.

Chapter 5

Ontological Justice as Racial Justice

The master's house has a beautiful façade of individual freedom and universal human equality. It is a façade that has become increasingly polished over time. But the master's house was built upon and remains on the same foundation of white supremacy. This is not to say that the advancements U.S. law has made in equality are meaningless. These have been advances hard-won by the immeasurable sacrifices of countless people. But at every junction, when change threatened the foundation, (white) America pivoted so that change would be reflected on the façade while safeguarding the white supremacy undergirding it all. It is not hard in the present-day United States to say that our legal system is just and equitable. The laws clearly state that individuals should not be treated differently on the basis of their race. It is also not hard to blame any racial disparities on either bad apples who should be held accountable for their bad acts or the victims themselves by holding that disparities are the result of individual choices made by people who refuse to take the steps needed to benefit from the bounty of our meritocratic system.

It is no surprise that the idea of critical race theory is so threatening to so many today. Any approach that invites us to look beyond the façade and explore the foundation of this house we all inhabit threatens to expose the façade and the foundation for what they truly are. And what would it mean to have an America not founded on white supremacy? What would it mean to have an America founded instead on the ideals it claims to espouse? This would entail taking the means necessary to dismantle the mechanisms that privilege whiteness at the expense of people of color, especially Black persons. This would mean nothing more than extending our ideals to their natural end, which is, sadly, a radical thing to suggest.

In his concurrence in *Adarand*, Scalia argued:

To pursue the concept of racial entitlement—even for the most admirable and
benign of purposes—is to reinforce and preserve for future mischief the way of
thinking that produced race slavery, race privilege and race hatred. In the eyes
of government, we are just one race here. It is American.[1]

This is illuminating. The thought that in the eyes of U.S. law, we are just
one race—American—is a nice one to have. It sounds in the fundamental
equality Jefferson (should have) addressed. It echoes Martin Luther King's *I
Have A Dream Speech*. But what exactly is racial entitlement? How does it
reinforce and preserve race privilege? What exactly is race privilege? And,
for that matter, does race privilege relate to race hatred and race slavery?
Scalia doesn't give us answers to these questions, but the message and its
logic are clear: to allow U.S. law to act in ways that benefit persons of color
now would be indistinguishable from the way U.S. law was allowed to act in
ways that benefited white persons during slavery and segregation. If it was
wrong for U.S. law to side with the whites then it is wrong for U.S. law to
side with the nonwhites now. U.S. law cannot pick winners and losers on the
basis of race.

The problem is that U.S. law already has. Since the beginning, U.S. law
has reinforced and preserved entitlements and privileges for white persons
at the expense of persons of color, especially Black persons. And so, when
Scalia, in that very same concurrence, unequivocally proclaims that "individuals who have been wronged by unlawful racial discrimination should
be made whole," he knows he has to immediately close those windows and
lock the doors: "Individuals who have been wronged by unlawful racial discrimination should be made whole; but under our Constitution there can be
no such thing as either a creditor or a debtor race. That concept is alien to
the Constitution's focus upon the individual."[2] And there it is. The sound of
a door weighing 400 years slamming shut. Before U.S. law, only individuals
exist. Whiteness and blackness are not real. Blackness cannot be wronged.
Whiteness can never be to blame. This is the crux of power, privilege, and
white supremacy in our colorblind world. U.S. law was wielded to create this
(white) America, and U.S. law can be wielded to replace it with the America
we claim to be. To do so, however, will require nothing less than an ontological revolution.[3]

(White) America was made and is maintained through law.[4] Throughout
American history, U.S. law has consistently claimed to safeguard equality
and liberty for all persons while doing so only for those enjoying the privilege of getting to count as persons truly. U.S. law has been instrumental in
creating and maintaining a world by and for white persons, a (white) America
in which persons of color, especially Black persons, have been devalued,
exploited, and kept in that subordinate status under the constant threat of

violence and death. At its inception, the United States was an expressly white supremacist project, and, despite significant changes, current U.S. law continues to safeguard white supremacy by concealing the tool nature of race beneath a false ontology.

Race is the tool that created and privileged whiteness by branding all non-Europeans as subordinate persons. The brand of blackness, applied to persons of African descent, was especially pernicious, relegating Black persons to the bottom rung of humanity. In the United States, law created the brand of race and has helped maintain it in continuous operation. Because the ontological branding function of race is about creating and maintaining white supremacy, the problem of racial injustice is about racial power inequalities, and the solution requires dismantling the mechanisms that privilege whiteness and subordinate persons of color.

But U.S. law denies the existence of racial power inequalities and instead approaches racial injustice as the ascription of significance to the insignificant fact of race. Because all individuals are equal before the law, current U.S. law holds, the problem arises if the law treats individuals differently on the basis of their race, and the solution is thus ensuring that the law disregards race and treats everyone the same way. Looking out onto a (white) America in which gross racial disparities are the norm, U.S. law largely considers these disparities to equal the sum of private choices by individuals of all racial groups and not the result of the law's own participation in maintaining white supremacy. By dismissing race as a meaningless fact, U.S. law thus conceals the tool nature of race and defines away the ontological inequality between white and nonwhite persons. As Mills explains, where once it was denied that persons of color were persons at all, "it is now pretended that nonwhites are equal abstract persons who can be fully included in the polity... without any fundamental change in the arrangements that have resulted from the previous system of explicit de jure racial privilege."[5] The net result is a legal system that, despite significant changes, continues to safeguard white supremacy by devaluing and exploiting persons of color, especially Black persons, and subjecting them to the constant threat of violence and death.

Instead of turning a blind eye to race, racial justice requires, in the words of Justice Sotomayor, "to speak openly and candidly on the subject of race, and to apply the Constitution with eyes open to the unfortunate effects of centuries of racial discrimination."[6] These unfortunate effects include the ontological subordination of persons of color for the sake of privileging white persons within the white supremacist world that is (white) America. These open eyes recognize that "race is a social construct" is a truism that cannot be equated with "race is not real." As Robin Dembroff notes in their analysis of social ontology, "[w]hile social kinds are 'up to us' in the thin sense that they ontologically depend on social structures and practices, we cannot revise, create, or destroy them through mere desire, thought, or assertion. To revise social kinds, we must revise material structures and practices."[7] In other words, there can be no racial equality without ontological equality, no individual freedom without ontological freedom. Racial justice requires ontological justice and should be understood, in the words of Judith Butler, as "not a matter of a simple entry of the excluded into an established ontology, but an insurrection at the level of ontology, a critical opening up of the questions, what is real? Whose lives are real? How might reality be remade?"[8] The end game is not a colorblind version of (white) America but the building of an America that truly lives up to its promises of equality and liberty for all, even and especially at an ontological level.

In MacKinnon's classic formulation, "inequality is not a matter of sameness and difference, but of dominance and subordination. Inequality is about power, its definition, and its maldistribution."[9] Because racial inequality is about racial dominance, racial injustice is about ontological control, and our approach to racial justice must shift to focus on ontology. Racial injustice must be reimagined as primarily about participation in an ongoing system of ontological brandedness.[10] This can have a dimension of morality or animus—the deliberate subordination of persons of color and the deliberate privileging of whiteness, as current U.S. law imagines racial animus—but it need not. Understanding racial injustice as participation in the ongoing subordination of persons of color and privileging of whiteness accounts for social and institutional forms of racial oppression. We can—and do—all participate in perpetuating ontological brands by simply being in (white) America and not affirmatively challenging it.[11] Racial injustice concerns the entrenched, universal, and invisible norms of white supremacy, and fighting for racial justice entails violating these norms to center those who are supposed to be marginalized and make conspicuous what is supposed to be the inconspicuous whiteness of the world.[12]

Racial justice will require, as Peller notes, a critical race consciousness.[13] Such a consciousness accepts that, as Yancy puts it, we are not "just simply influenced by racist practices, but [we are] the vehicle through which such practices get performed and maintained."[14] It is our participation that keeps this unjust system going. Yancy notes, "[t]o be white in America is to be always already implicated in structures of power."[15] And because in America "one is always already complicit with whiteness,"[16] to be American is to be always already implicated in white supremacy because "racist actions are also habits of the body and not simply cognitively false beliefs."[17] Racial injustice recedes into the invisible background of ordinary everydayness for most of us because in (white) America, privileging whiteness and subordinating non-whiteness is what we do.[18] This understanding of white privilege and white supremacy do not require that we understand all white persons to be culpable or equally so. As Mills notes, "some may be both actors and beneficiaries while others are just beneficiaries."[19]

Current U.S. law provides an effective smokescreen against these phenomena. By focusing on combatting specific acts of intentional discrimination by particular individuals, current U.S. law equates racial injustice with individual racism. As Mills writes, however, "the real issue for a long time has not been individual racism but, far more important, the reproduction of wrongful white advantage and unjust nonwhite (particularly Black and Latino) disadvantage through the workings of racialized social structures."[20] It is thus important to note, as MacKinnon did in a feminist context, that "[p]ractices of inequality need not be intentionally discriminatory. The status quo need only be reflected unchanged."[21] Our status quo—(white) America— is a world that privileges whiteness, and, like any world, its maintenance is predicated on our collective, continued participation.[22] To truly move toward racial justice, we must thus move toward dismantling white privilege, and this will only be possible by starving this (white) world of the participation in ontological privilege and subordination on which it depends.[23] Antiracism on an ontological level "must come in the form of a continuously affirmed refusal to prolong the ontological and existential project of whiteness."[24] There is no specific finish line, no single reparations payout, and no law to pass that will make this project complete.[25]

This has unsettling implications for the unbranded. There is a "difficult but inevitable issue of what whites should do with the racial power they actually possess; not exercising this power affirmatively does not make it disappear."[26] In fact, a proper understanding of the ontological oppression inherent in race reveals that the liberalist myth is itself implicated. We are not and can never be self-constructed individuals. We are always already in worlds, and our identity is a dance between chosen and unchosen dimensions of ourselves. The antiracist person, particularly the antiracist white person, "is not an atomic self but a deeply historically embedded self,"[27] and "undoing whiteness is inextricably linked to undoing those structural power relationships that continue to privilege whites, even as they strive to perform whiteness differently within the context of transacting with people of color on a daily basis."[28]

MAKING THE INVISIBLE VISIBLE

As U.S. law turns a blind eye to race, it turns a blind eye to the ongoing ontological harm exacted upon persons of color, especially Black persons, in (white) America. But law's refusal to protect someone from harm is just another name for law protecting another's right to cause that harm. And this brings us back to the very beginning. U.S. law continues to protect a right to harm persons of color, especially Black persons, and this right to harm is the foundation of white privilege in (white) America.[29] That ontological harm is legally unrecognized is unsurprising considering that the only persons who experience ontological harm are those excluded from full participation in the (unbranded) world. Because ontological branding works precisely to manufacture power inequalities, ontological harm flows only in one direction: against the branded. As regards race, there is no ontological harm that could be suffered by a white person in (white) America; whiteness is defined by the privilege to harm persons of color.

Peller's work helpfully illuminates this dynamic. Discussing sexual harassment as an example, Peller notes that even though sexual harassment constitutes a harm "that is widely recognized as an injury in our culture," there is no American jurisdiction that recognizes a general common law right, as opposed to a statutory right, "to recovery for injury from sexual harassment."[30] In other words,

> harassers have a common law privilege to sexually harass, and victims have no right with respect to the harassment. The state will not protect the victims from the harm, require the party causing the harm to pay compensation, or permit self-help that would violate any legally protected interests of the party causing the harm. . . . Sexual harassment constitutes a damnum absque injuria region of privilege that is in turn a factor in the gendered distribution of power and wealth. The privilege to harass forms the baseline from which any further transactions must proceed. [31]

A similar structure operates vis-à-vis ontological brandedness and race. Ontological harm currently constitutes a damnum absque injuria region of privilege that is, in turn, a factor in the racialized distribution of power and wealth. The privilege to treat persons of color as ontologically subordinate forms a baseline for action within (white) America.

U.S. law avoids addressing much of the racial injustice operant today—viz., the baseline right to harm persons of color—by placing it within the realm of the private sphere. While U.S. law largely prohibits governmental action that discriminates on the basis of race, the law recognizes a private right to do so, even out of discriminatory animus. This brings us back to the scenario where societal inequalities along racial lines are understood to be an effect of private choices and thus permissible, instead of being understood as the result of state power wielded in the interests of white supremacy and thus impermissible. But, as Peller argues,

> [i]nequality of fortune is not the result of free choice in a private property regime, it is a function of, and built into, the legal regime within which parties interact. . . . The private sphere is constituted by governmental decisions about

the distribution of rights and privileges, which in turn form the context for any "private" transactions. There is no way for the state simply to leave an issue to the market by declining to recognize a claim because the failure to recognize a right simply creates a different jural relationship and thereby regulates the parties in a different way.[32]

Accordingly, Peller states that "the colorblindness baseline can be seen to describe a realm of racial damnum absque injuria, in which actors are privileged to inflict the injury of disproportionate impact on African-Americans who have no right to stop the practice in question."[33] U.S. law has "recognized a privilege on the part of state actors to act . . . without regard to the impact on racial minority communities, and thereby to inflict harm on members of those communities."[34]

White privilege is ontological; it is the right to cause ontological harm. It is not the case that a white person has the right to go out and punch a Black person. At least not entirely. In that scenario, the Black person being punched has legal recourse for battery and several other possible claims because U.S. law will protect everyone from battery, and no one has the right to batter. There is, of course, the MacKinnon and Zack realist observations that there is significant distance between the rights that white and Black persons equally enjoy in theory and the ones they enjoy, in fact. A white person punching a white person and a Black person punching a white person would likely face very different outcomes. And it is in this difference in outcomes that ontological disparities begin to be disclosed. In (white) America, Black lives matter less. Because of this, at every step through the chain of events that need to unfold between the punching of a face to a criminal sentence or a jury award, a Black person will move through the world encumbered, devalued, and always subject to the threat of violence or death while their white counterpart simply will not.

In the end, in a (white) America where white persons hold the lion's share of power to control and shape a world by and for them, persons of color can be marginalized, their interests silenced, and their harms ignored.[35] As Peller puts it, discussing affirmative action as an example,

> Limiting the baseline definition of racial injustice to the intentional use of race, affirmative action appears as an intervention in an otherwise racially neutral realm. But that conception obscures the associated recognition of a legal privilege to engage in conduct having a racially disproportionate impact, a privilege that helps to construct the distribution of wealth, power, and prestige among racial groups.[36]

To challenge the ontological privilege enjoyed by whiteness, we might reimagine "multiculturalism" in the United States as a complex of worlds, each with its boundaries and integrity.[37] As Peller proposes, "imagine a sophisticated vision of racial justice that would systematically replace the individualist focus ... with a focus on cultural communities and would simultaneously view institutional practices as a reflection of particular manifestations of cultural power."[38] Under this system, as MacKinnon writes in the context of gender, "[t]he intent requirement would be eliminated... Statistical proofs of disparity would be conclusive. The main question would be: does a practice participate in the subordination of women to men, or is it no part of it?"[39] And, in the context of race, as Peller describes, "[t]he racially identifiable results of a purportedly neutral selection procedure are simply taken as more reliable evidence of racial bias than the vague and subjective inquiry into intent."[40]

While our legal approach to racial justice has shifted toward colorblindness, it should instead shift toward the very race-conscious dismantling of white privilege.[41] What is needed is a disruption of the process of ontological oppression, a dismantling of the mechanisms that so naturally create and maintain ontological brands.[42] This will require treating unalikes unalike in order to make them alike.[43]

CREATING ONTOLOGICAL EQUALITY

Under the naïve, folktale model of racism, racial justice means colorblindness because it means treating all persons equally regardless of race.[44] But a proper understanding of the ontological dimension of race discloses that racial groups are not ontologically equal.[45] Racial injustice is neither power neutral nor equidirectional among racial groups, and it is best understood as participation, express or tacit, in an ongoing system of ontological subordination and privilege. As Mills puts it, "[r]acial injustice is, most fundamentally, a refusal to respect equal personhood, whether in the original rights-violations or in the legacy of such violations."[46] Understanding race as ontological brand helps us keep our focus on the power inequality inherent in race. The fundamental legal question concerning racial justice is thus not whether U.S. law is treating all individuals equally but whether U.S. law is being used to support or dismantle white supremacy.

In (white) America, white and nonwhite persons are not equal. A white person moves ontologically unencumbered as a person simpliciter in a world by and for persons. Persons of color, however, are encumbered by their ontological brands and restricted to ways of being that serve the interests of that white world. Colorblindness as racial justice is predicated on an ontological lie.[47] By denying that white persons and persons of color are subject to separate and unequal ways of being (allowed to be) in (white)

America, U.S. law "ignores the differential advantages and privileges that have accumulated in the white population because of the past history of discrimination,"[48] and advances colorblindness "as another way of avoiding challenging white structural power."[49] By defining away ontological inequalities between white and nonwhite persons, U.S. law is assuming the situation really is equal in order to make it so, but, as MacKinnon noted, this is no more than "the sentimentality of liberalism" because it "misdiagnoses the stake the dominant have in maintaining the situation, because neither it nor they know they are dominant."[50] Colorblindness, precisely under the ostensible banner of racial justice, turns out to be a trojan horse for white supremacy.[51]

In her dissent in *Schuette*, Justice Sotomayor argued that

> Protecting the right to meaningful participation in the political process must mean more than simply removing barriers to participation. It must mean vigilantly policing the political process to ensure that the majority does not use other methods to prevent minority groups from partaking in that process on equal footing.[52]

But persons of color are not on equal ontological footing with white persons, and racial justice will require an acknowledgment of this reality—an acknowledgment of the oppressive mechanics inherent in a racialized system as a first step toward dismantling the ways in which nonwhiteness is encumbered and whiteness privileged thereby.[53] Because whiteness and nonwhiteness are ontologically unalike due to the ontological power wielded by U.S. law, whiteness and nonwhiteness must be treated in unalike manners precisely to correct the inequalities that have accumulated in (white) America. Because racial groups are not ontologically equal, racial justice as safeguarding equality among individuals regardless of race does not work.[54] Racial groups are not alike, and treating unalikes alike is as unjust as treating likes unalike.[55] Racial justice instead requires treating the unalikes unalike for the sake of making them alike truly.

This can sound crazy to the ears of current U.S. law, but this is not a new concept. In his concurrence in *California v. Bakke*, Justice Harry Blackmun expressly noted that "[i]n order to get beyond racism, we must first take account of race. There is no other way. And in order to treat some persons equally, we must treat them differently."[56] And outside of the racial context, U.S. law routinely recognizes that unalike persons need to be treated in unalike manners precisely because we want them to be alike. Consider the concepts of accessibility and accommodations within the Americans with Disabilities Act. The foundation of disability law is the understanding that because there should be equality between persons who are disabled and those who are not, U.S. law will take existing inequalities into account to require measures to make the unequal equal.

Consider, for example, an accessibility ramp. It is because we recognize that persons who can walk stairs and persons who cannot walk stairs should have equal access to the same buildings that we require affirmative measures to ensure that buildings are accessible to persons in wheelchairs. U.S law also requires reasonable accommodations for persons with disabilities. In the employment context, for example, the ADA requires an employer "to provide reasonable accommodation" to persons with disabilities. An "accommodation" is defined as "any change in the work environment or in the way things are customarily done that enables an individual with a disability to enjoy equal employment opportunities." As the U.S. Equal Employment Opportunity Commission explains:

> The duty to provide reasonable accommodation is a fundamental statutory requirement because of the nature of discrimination faced by individuals with disabilities. Although many individuals with disabilities can apply for and perform jobs without any reasonable accommodations, there are workplace barriers that keep others from performing jobs which they could do with some form of accommodation. These barriers may be physical obstacles (such as inaccessible facilities or equipment), or they may be procedures or rules (such as rules concerning when work is performed, when breaks are taken, or how essential or marginal functions are performed). Reasonable accommodation removes workplace barriers for individuals with disabilities.[57]

In the context of inequalities caused by disabilities, U.S. law recognizes that while creating access to otherwise inaccessible spaces is essential, the "nature" of discrimination that persons with disabilities face is unique and requires more than just access; it requires spaces to affirmatively change "the environment" and "the way things are customarily done" to remove "barriers" in the form of "obstacles," "procedures," or "rules." By acknowledging the inequality faced by persons with disabilities in a world made by and for those without disabilities, U.S. law is able to treat persons with disabilities differently to begin to turn an (ableist) America into an America by and for all.

U.S. law understands discrimination in the disability context to be not (only) about bad people wishing to exclude disabled persons but far more simply about whether persons with disabilities can meaningfully access and participate in a world in which they have experienced a "history and pattern of unequal treatment."[58] To have U.S. law instead focus on guaranteeing that everyone is treated the same way without regard to disability in the interest of equality would be worse than nonsensical; it would disclose bad faith.[59] This fundamental idea—that, in the face of underlying inequalities, unequal treatment is exactly what we need because persons should be equal—is what a critical race consciousness brings to the table once the ontology underlying race is properly disclosed. Justice Sotomayor urged the Court to adopt this type of consciousness in the dimension of race.

> We often think of equal protection as a guarantee that the government will apply the law in an equal fashion—that it will not intentionally discriminate against minority groups. But equal protection of the laws means more than that; it also secures the right of all citizens to participate meaningfully and equally in the process through which laws are created.
>
> Few rights are as fundamental as the right to participate meaningfully and equally in the process of governance.[60]

Within a white supremacist world, the brand of nonwhiteness operates in many ways, like a disability. Note, for example, the uncanny similarities between the injustices faced by nonwhite persons and those faced by disabled persons, as described by the U.S. Supreme Court in *Tennessee v. Lane* 541 US 509 (2004):

> It is not difficult to perceive the harm that Title II is designed to address. Congress enacted Title II against a backdrop of pervasive unequal treatment in the administration of state services and programs, including systematic deprivations of fundamental rights. . . . The historical experience that Title II reflects is also documented in this Court's cases, which have identified unconstitutional treatment of disabled persons by state agencies in a variety of settings, including unjustified commitment, the abuse and neglect of persons committed to state mental health hospitals, and irrational discrimination in zoning decisions. The decisions of other courts, too, document a pattern of unequal treatment in the administration of a wide range of public services, programs, and activities, including the penal system, public education, and voting. Notably, these decisions also demonstrate a pattern of unconstitutional treatment in the administration of justice.[61]

The nonwhite person has restricted access to the shared world, and, even to the degree there is access, the nonwhite person is prevented from meaningfully participating. A critical race consciousness that takes this into account would, as Justice Sotomayor argues, recognize that the Constitution "guarantees that the majority may not win by stacking the political process against minority groups permanently, forcing the minority alone to surmount unique obstacles in pursuit of its goals."[62]

Nonwhite persons have been excluded from white spaces and excluded from the institutions that control and shape (white) America. To truly begin to move toward ontological equality requires creating the equivalent of access ramps specifically designed for persons of color, i.e., race-conscious measures taken specifically for persons of color to access these spaces. More than that, it requires an acknowledgment that the reason why white spaces are white, especially in seats of power, is because of 400 years of state-sponsored subordination of persons of color. Persons of color are being denied access and prevented from meaningfully participating in white spaces the way they have always been. Given the history and pattern of ongoing discrimination faced by persons of color within (white) America, the presumption should thus be that white spaces are white because of exclusion.

Understanding racial justice in terms of ontological justice reframes our understanding of race-conscious affirmative action measures. For example, instead of banning racial quotas for the sake of preventing discrimination, U.S. law would approach racial quotas as accessibility measures precisely to protect against discrimination. The underrepresentation of persons of color (and the overrepresentation of white persons) across contemporary American power-wielding institutions is the harvest of white privilege and racial subordination. To hold that U.S. law will be blind to claims of racial harm as such is to continue in the fallacy MacKinnon pointed out a generation ago in the feminist context: injuries shared by most if not all of a group means that no individual "is differentially injured enough to be able to sue for [the] deepest injuries,"[63] i.e., ontological injuries. These injuries are permissible under our current legal system given the broader, hidden project of protecting white privilege and maintaining white supremacy in (white) America. Were our legal system instead to recognize the ontological dimensions of racial oppression, a state interest, if not a constitutional requirement to dismantle white supremacy would follow, and affirmatively busting up the cartels of historically white spaces would be common sense.

Ontological justice entails redressing the encumbrance of branded persons, removing restrictions on the ways branded persons are allowed to be in the world. In the contemporary American racial context, this entails, to start, recognition by our legal system that persons of color are ontologically subordinated and that white persons are privileged thereby. This also entails the legal recognition that because a formal commitment to disregard race will do nothing to change this, state action is needed to affirmatively place persons of color in the power-wielding institutions to which access has been restricted, not only as a manner of redressing past wrongs but as a way to proactively seed the dismantling of an ongoing system that privileges whiteness.

To recognize a right to ontological equality is to recognize that white spaces need to move toward becoming inclusive spaces representative of the racial diversity we see in America. This is an ontological revolution because it entails U.S. law recognizing the tool nature of race. It entails U.S. law recognizing the reality of ontological subordination of nonwhiteness for the sake of privileging whiteness within (white) America. It entails U.S. law recognizing its own critical role in that story. And it entails an acknowledgment of ontological power more broadly, including the various ways different groups of persons are subordinated for the sake of privileging the unbranded as the true masters and makers of our shared world.

NOTES

1. *Adarand* 239.
2. *Adarand* 239.
3. Warren, *Ontological Terror*, 171.
4. Warren, *Ontological Terror*, 66, 77 (discussing the role law plays in shaping ontologies).
5. Mills, *Racial Contract*, 75.
6. *Schuette* 381.
7. Dembroff, "Real Talk on the Metaphysics of Gender", 24.
8. Judith Butler, *Precarious Life: The Powers of Mourning and Violence* (London: Verso, 2004), 33.
9. MacKinnon, *Toward a Feminist Theory of the State*, 242.
10. Mills, *Racial Contract*, 107 (arguing that "[b]y unquestioningly "going along with things," by accepting all the privileges of whiteness with concomitant complicity in the system of white supremacy, one can be said to have consented to whiteness.").
11. MacKinnon, *Toward a Feminist Theory of the State*, 234 ("Practices of inequality need not be intentionally discriminatory. The status quo need only be reflected unchanged."); Mills, *Black Rights/ White Wrongs*, 37.
12. Andrea Gawrylewski, "The Case for Antiracism," *Scientific American*, Summer 2021 (describing racism as a moving walkway at the airport that will carry you along unless you walk, vigorously, in the other direction).
13. Peller, *Critical Race Consciousness*.
14. Yancy, *Black Bodies, White Gazes*, 39.
15. Yancy, *Black Bodies, White Gazes*, 226.
16. Yancy, *Black Bodies, White Gazes*, 221.
17. Yancy, *Black Bodies, White Gazes*, 39.
18. Rothstein, *Color of Law*, 55; Natapoff, *Punishment Without Crime*, 8; Manne, Kate, "Humanism," *Social Theory and Practice* 42, no. 2 (2016): 389–415, 406–407; Taylor, J. *Techno-Racism*.
19. Mills, *Black Rights/ White Wrongs*, 121. See Yancy, *Black Bodies, White Gazes*, 42 (discussing how there is no need to hold racist beliefs to be a beneficiary of whiteness); Kendi, *Stamped from the Beginning*, 10 (distinguishing between producers and consumers of racist ideas).
20. Mills, *Black Rights/ White Wrongs*, 118.
21. MacKinnon, *Toward a Feminist Theory of the State*, 234.
22. See Mills, *Racial Contract*, 37. The world of (white) America can be understood as a biopolitical network, where "[b]iopolitical networks rely for their stability

and growth upon our engagement in self-policing, upon our willingness to discipline ourselves and those around us to meet the standards of function and the direction of development that our assigned roles specify." McWhorter, *Racism and Sexual Oppression in Anglo-America*, 325.

23. McWhorter, *Racism and Sexual Oppression in Anglo-America*, 326 (to move "toward dismantling biopolitical... networks of power, therefore, is to refuse to do the work for them, to refuse to do the work of self- (and other-) policing in the name of the normal."). See Peller, *Critical Race Consciousness*, 59 (discussing the Malcolm X approach to Black nationalism as focused on the "dismantling of power relations between white and Black communities.").

24. Yancy, *Black Bodies, White Gazes*, 222.

25. Yancy, *Black Bodies, White Gazes*, 219 ("Rather than rest assured she is fighting white privilege, when engaging in resistance a person needs to continually be questioning the effects of her activism on both self and world.").

26. Peller, *Critical Race Consciousness*, 103; Yancy, *Black Bodies, White Gazes*, 41("Benefiting from acting whitely in the world can have negative implications for nonwhites, even if whites are unaware of the consequences of their actions.").

27. Yancy, *Black Bodies, White Gazes*, 256.

28. Yancy, *Black Bodies, White Gazes*, 233. Note that recognizing that whiteness enjoys an unjust ontological privilege does not imply that the (white) world is bad in se. Further, despite the fact that ontological justice may feel like a loss of rights for the ontologically privileged, this does not mean that ontological justice on the racial dimension requires demoting whiteness. Racial justice on an existential level entails that "Blacks must negate the ideological structure of whiteness" within which Black persons have been forced to operate, but "Black identity does not have as its ontological aim the negation of white people." Yancy, *Black Bodies, White Gazes*, 113.

29. Peller, "Privilege," 895–900.

30. Peller, "Privilege," 900.

31. Peller, "Privilege," 900.

32. Peller, "Privilege," 903; Peller, *Critical Race Consciousness*, 124.

33. Peller, "Privilege," 914. To illustrate this privilege as a right-to-harm dynamic in a gender context, Peller takes pornography as an example. In the terms used in this paper, pornography could be understood to inflict ontological harm on women given, e.g. "the harm it causes women in terms of the social and cultural perception of them." Peller, Privilege 912. But "[t]o the extent that men have this privilege, women have no right with respect to the harm inflicted; were they to use self-help to avoid this harm, the state would act to protect the pornographers from harm to any of their legally protected interests." Peller, "Privilege," 912. Ultimately, "[b]ecause the harm from pornography is not traditionally recognized in the common law categories, it is easy to assume that there is simply no harm at all." Peller, "Privilege," 912.

34. Peller, "Privilege," 915.

35. Peller, "Privilege," 893 (citations omitted). It is no surprise that Black nationalism has been vilified by (white) America. As Peller puts it, "Black nationalism embodied a profound rejection of the reigning ideology for understanding the distribution of power and privilege in American society." Peller, *Critical Race Consciousness*, 23. In

other words, Black nationalism was an extreme form of collective Black uppitiness, challenging the brand of Black as ontologically ersatz and directly threatening white privilege thereby.

36. Peller, "Privilege," 887.
37. Alcoff, *Visible Identities*.
38. Peller, *Critical Race Consciousness*, 46.
39. MacKinnon, *Toward a Feminist Theory of the State*, 248.
40. Peller, *Critical Race Consciousness*, 46.
41. Colorblindness and eliminativism are the natural results of Rawlsean approaches. Mills, *Black Rights/ White Wrongs*, 157, 158.
42. Mills, *Black Rights/ White Wrongs*, 159.
43. Cf. MacKinnon, *Toward a Feminist Theory of the State*, 224 ("Why should one have to be the same as a man to get what a man gets simply because he is one?").
44. Cf. Manne, *Down Girl*, 63–64 (arguing that misogyny targets women because they are women in a man's world not women in a man's mind).
45. Cf. Peller, *Critical Race Consciousness*, 23 ("The equation of Black nationalists and white supremacists assumes a neutral standard from which to identify race consciousness as a deviation and link race inherently to prejudice and domination.")
46. *Racial injustice is anti-liberal."* Mills, *Black Rights/ White Wrongs*, 178.
47. See Peller, "Privilege," 920 (noting that "the deeper problem with the old order was that its claims about the nature and character of our social lives were false—classical legal thought presented inequality as if it were simply the result of the exercise of rights that everyone enjoyed, and suppressed the role of social and collective power embodied in legal rules that benefited some at the expense of others. . . . [T]here is no neutral way to avoid law's construction of racial power by pursuing "colorblind" policies.").
48. Mills, *Black Rights/ White Wrongs*, 159.
49. Yancy, *Black Bodies, White Gazes*, 225.
50. MacKinnon, *Toward a Feminist Theory of the State*, 231.
51. Mills, *Racial Contract*, 76; Natapoff, *Punishment Without Crime,* 159 (noting that "a great deal of racially skewed decision-making is neither acknowledged by, nor amenable to change under, current constitutional law"); López 70 (noting that "the current Court uses the Constitution to protect the racial status quo: it principally condones discrimination against minorities, and virtually always condemns efforts to achieve greater racial equality.").
52. *Schuette* 369.
53. Racial justice is "not pre-emptive measures to prevent racial injustice but corrective measures to rectify injustices *that have already occurred."* Mills, *Black Rights/ White Wrongs*, 162. See Polizzi, *A Phenomenological Hermeneutic*, 17 (addressing the myth of individualism and noting the per se social nature of human existence). Because in reality disparities exist between Black and white ways of being (allowed to be) in the (white) world, a postracialist frame leads people to the seemingly natural conclusion that blackness is itself the cause of this disparity: if racism is a thing of the past, and if our legal system is largely colorblind, our lot in life is largely of our own making. The net result is a white supremacist system that understands itself as

colorblind and postracial. See MacKinnon, *Toward a Feminist Theory of the State*, 215; Kendi, *Stamped from the Beginning*, 499; Yancy, *Black Bodies, White Gazes*, 226; Sumi Cho, *Postracialism*.

When people are acting within their determined roles, it is easy to say that we are on the side of racial justice. "It is so easy to hide behind antiracist rhetoric when one limits oneself to predictable social encounters that are already predicated upon social transactions that do not challenge or complicate the white self." Yancy, *Black Bodies, White Gazes*, 224. Barrack Obama is sometimes proffered as proof that racism is dead. Paradoxically, however, Barrack Obama turned out to be the ideal candidate for preserving white supremacy. Kendi, *Stamped from the Beginning*, 483. By being the embodiment of the "extraordinary negro" who was also very careful to not rock the racial boat, the unbranded could support his ascent and thereby feel that they were the embodiment of racial justice. When Obama was elected, the unbranded could claim that racism was dead and that we could finally end the conversation on racial discrimination and move forward in our post-racial world.

54. Rothstein, *Color of Law*, 189 (arguing that government actions "cannot be neutral about segregation. They will either exacerbate or reverse it.").

55. MacKinnon, *Toward a Feminist Theory of the State*, 231 ("To suppose that legally assuming the situation really is equal in order to make it so is the sentimentality of liberalism.").

56. *Regents of the University of California v. Bakke* 438 US 265, 407 (1978). Blackmun concurrence.

57. United States Equal Employment Opportunity Commission, "Enforcement Guidance on Reasonable Accommodation and Undue Hardship under the ADA," *Notice No. 915.002* October 17, 2002 available at https://www.eeoc.gov/laws/guidance/enforcement-guidance-reasonable-accommodation-and-undue-hardship-under-ada#general.

58. *Tennessee v. Lane*, 541 U.S. 509 (2004).

59. Mills, *Racial Contract*, 98, quoting Lewis Gordon.

60. *Schuette* 365–366.

61. *Tennessee v. Lane* 541 US 509, 525 (2004) (internal citations omitted).

62. *Schuette* 342.

63. MacKinnon, *Toward a Feminist Theory of the State*, 239.

Conclusion

(White) America is a world in which persons of color, especially Black persons, are devalued, exploited, and subject to a constant threat of violence and death for the sake of privileging white persons as the true *We* of *We the People*. The privilege of whiteness entails getting to be a person simpliciter in a world by and for equal persons. Most fundamentally, personhood in a liberal democracy means getting to be an end in oneself and enjoying the broad freedom to determine one's ways of being in the world. The privilege of whiteness is created by subordinating nonwhiteness. Persons of color are excluded from full participation in personhood and are instead relegated to subordinate person status. Persons of color are not ends in themselves and can be treated as means toward the end of supporting the (white) world. When persons of color remain within the spaces permitted them by the (white) world, they fade into the inconspicuous background of that (white) world where white lives are foregrounded. When persons of color move outside those confines, i.e., when persons of color transgress the boundaries between whiteness and nonwhiteness, they become hypervisible to the white gaze, obtrusive in the (white) world, and invite punishment.

Whiteness was created by ontologically branding non-Europeans as subordinate beings. In the United States, persons of African descent were all branded with the same brand of blackness that designated them as the quintessential subordinate beings. Black persons were thus excluded from full participation in personhood and were instead reduced to roles in service to (white) America. The boundary between whiteness and blackness began with U.S. law creating a white right to harm Black persons. This right to harm existed to exploit Black persons and punish them for stepping outside their permitted spaces. This right to harm is the foundation of white privilege, a privilege that U.S. law continues to protect.

In antebellum America, U.S. law protected the right to enslave Black persons and the right to punish those who attempted to free themselves. That white supremacist system was (1) justified through an explicit legal belief that non-Europeans, especially those of African descent, were beings of an inferior order whose inferiority justified their enslavement; and (2) maintained by subjecting Black persons to the constant threat of violence and death.

In Jim Crow America, U.S. law protected the right to segregate Black persons into particular enclaves, exclude Black persons from areas of socioeconomic development, constrain Black persons to service roles, and punish Black persons who attempted to challenge those constraints. That white supremacist system was (1) justified through an explicit legal belief that while the law required that white and Black persons be given formally equal treatment, white and Black persons were unequal by nature; and (2) maintained by subjecting Black persons to the constant threat of violence and death.

In colorblind America, U.S. law continues to protect the right to devalue and exploit the lives of people of color, especially Black lives, by, inter alia, safeguarding white control over (white) America. This white supremacist system is (1) justified through an explicit legal belief that while the law requires that persons be given equal governmental treatment regardless of race, the law is powerless to intervene in societal discrimination caused by private choices; and (2) maintained by subjecting persons of color, especially Black persons, to the constant threat of violence and death through, inter alia, pretextual incarceration and extrajudicial killings.

White privilege began by protecting a white person's right to harm Black persons. In the beginning, this was a de jure individual right: an individual white person could harm an individual Black person, and the law would not recognize that harm as harm at all; the law would intervene only to prevent the Black person from resorting to self-defense. In colorblind (white) America, whatever de jure right to harm a white individual once enjoyed no longer exists, but white privilege and the right to harm persons of color, especially Black persons, remains the backbone of American white supremacy. The difference is that the right to harm is now collective. This right is now exercised in the everyday workings of a (white) world that routinely marginalizes, exploits, and threatens communities of color. U.S. law protects this right and helps maintain the power to shape (white) America in white hands. The result is vast racial disparities within a purportedly colorblind world. The justification is a focus on the individual and holding the individual as sacrosanct because all are created equal, and all have an equal stake in the cocreating of this shared world. That this sleight of hand is as effective as it is bears witness to the success of 400 years of subordination that have created a (white)

America in which white supremacy has become the inconspicuous presence of the world itself.

In this (white) America, while an individual white person and an individual Black person ostensibly face the exact same world subject to the same laws, one of them gets to be a proper person and one does not. One of them is an infinitely valuable end in themselves, moving through a world made by and for them as they pursue life, liberty, and happiness. The other is branded as subordinate, and every step of the way is expected to assume roles in service to that (white) world. At the end of the day, one of them will be in the (white) world as the person they are and look out at (white) America and be at home. The other will not be permitted to be in the (white) world in the same way and is instead condemned to a life at war, fighting for the freedom to simply be. This is the ontological dimension of subordination and privilege. This is the ontological dimension of white supremacy maintained through U.S. law.

The ontological privilege of unbrandedness in a world by and for the unbranded is getting to be a fish in water swimming downstream. To be unbranded is to be at home in a place where you can be who you are as you are. It is to move with the lightness of being in a place oriented toward you, and it is the privilege of not seeing or feeling the tremendous cost of human suffering that it takes to build that world. But to be branded in a world by and for the unbranded is to be swimming upstream. It is to have obstacles everywhere, especially where you are not supposed to go. It is to wear a suit of hooks that catch on the world constantly, holding you back, pulling you away from the forbidden ways of being. It is to be rewarded for knowing your place and staying in it. It is to be punished for failing to do so. It is to constantly live under the tension of being seen for the brand you bear and not for the person you are because you are invisible behind the roles you are supposed to play. If you play these roles, you fade into the background of a world that keeps the unbranded in the foreground of their stories. If you do not play your permitted roles and step beyond the confines of your permitted ways of being, your invisibility ends. You stick out. You are unruly, uppity. You invite being put back in your place, often violently.

Racial justice is about ontological justice. If justice is about equality and freedom, racial justice is about ontological equality and ontological freedom. Without an ontological revolution in U.S. law to recognize the white supremacy that U.S. law itself has made, it will be impossible to replace (white) America with the America we claim to be, an America in which little Black boys and Black girls will not only be able to join hands with little white boys and white girls as sisters and brothers but will be able to be in the world who they are, as they are, on their terms, and not on terms imposed on them by someone else's world.

This project began with a basic question: what is race? That simple question disclosed that what race is is inextricably linked with what race is for: race is a tool for creating and maintaining (white) America. But this raises other equally fundamental questions: what is America? What is America for? Who is America for? I hope that my project can provide language to help in the ongoing struggle to make America what it claims to be, an America by and for all of us.

Bibliography

SUPREME COURT DECISIONS

Adarand v. Peña, 515 US 200 (1995).
Dred Scott v. Sandford, 60 U.S. 393, 407 (1857).
Parents Involved in Community Schools v. Seattle School District No. 1, 551 US 701 (2007).
Plessy v. Ferguson, 163 U.S. 537, 544 (1896).
Regents of the University of California v. Bakke 438 US 265 (1978).
Schuette v. Coalition to Defend Affirmative Action, 572 US 291 (2014).
Tennessee v. Lane, 541 U.S. 509 (2004).

PUBLISHED LITERATURE

Ahmed, Sara. "A Phenomenology of Whiteness." *Feminist Theory* 8 (2007): 149–168.
———. *Queer Phenomenology: Orientations, Objects, Others* (Durham, NC: Duke University Press, 2006).
Alcoff, Linda Martín. *The Future of Whiteness* (Cambridge: Polity, 2015).
———. "Towards a Phenomenology of Racial Embodiment." *Radical Philosophy* 95 (1999): 15–26.
———. *Visible Identities: Race, Gender, and the Self* (Oxford: Oxford University Press, 2006).
Alexander, Michelle. *The New Jim Crow: Mass Incarceration in the Age of Colorblindness* (New York: The New Press, 2010).
Andrade, Sofia. "'Y yo no me voy a quedar callado': Anti-Blackness and Colorism in Miami's Latinx Community." *Harvard Political Review*, August 10, 2020.
Austin, Regina. "'The Shame of It All': Stigma and the Political Disenfranchisement of Formerly Convicted and Incarcerated Persons." *Columbia Human Rights Law Review* 36 (2004): 173.

Avraham, Ronen, and Kimberly Yuracko. "Torts and Discrimination." *Ohio State Law Journal* 78 (2017).
Baldwin, James. *I Am Not Your Negro*, edited by Raoul Peck (Paris: R. Laffont, 2017).
Balkin, Jack, and Reva Siegel. "Remembering How to Do Equality." In *The Constitution in 2020*, edited by Balkin and Siegel Siegel (Oxford: Oxford University Press, 2020).
Blattner, William. *Heidegger's Being and Time: A Reader's Guide* (London: Bloomsbury, 2006).
Bogel-Burroughs, Nicholas. "What We Learned on Day 2 of the Derek Chauvin Trial." *New York Times*, March 30, 2021.
Bowden, John. "Mitch McConnell Sparks Anger by Saying Black Americans 'Are Voting in Just as High a Percentage as Americans'." *Independent*, January 22, 2022.
Butler, Judith. *Precarious Life: The Powers of Mourning and Violence* (London: Verso, 2004).
Carbado, Devon W., and Cheryl I. Harris. "Intersectionality at 30: Mapping the Margins of Anti-Essentialism, Intersectionality, and Dominance Theory." *Harvard Law Review* 132 (2019): 2193.
Cherry, Myisha. "State Racism, State Violence, and Vulnerable Solidarity." In *The Oxford Handbook on Philosophy and Race*, edited by Naomi Zack (Oxford: Oxford University Press, 2017).
Cheryl Harris. "Whiteness as Property." *Harvard Law Review* 8 (June 1993): 106.
Chung, Andrew, Lawrence Hulrley, Botts Jackie, Andrea Januta, and Guillermo Gomez. "Shielded: For Cops Who Kill, Special Supreme Court Protection." *Reuters Investigates*, May 8, 2020.
Coates, Ta-Nehisi. *Between the World and Me* (New York: Spiegel & Grau, 2015).
———. "Trayvon Martin and the Irony of American Justice." *The Atlantic*, July 15, 2013.
Cudd, Anne E. *Analyzing Oppression* (Oxford: Oxford University Press, 2006).
De Pinto, Jennifer. "CBS News Poll: Widespread Agreement With Chauvin Verdict." *CBS News*, April 25, 2021.
Dembroff, Robin. "Real Talk on the Metaphysics of Gender." *Philosophical Topics* 46, no. 2 (Fall 2018): 21–50.
Dreyfus, Hubert. *Being-in-the-World: A Commentary on Heidegger's Being and Time, Division I* (Cambridge: MIT Press, 1991).
Du Bois, W. E. B. *Darkwater: Voices From Within the Veil* (New York: Harcourt, Brace, and Howe, 1920).
———. *The Souls of Black Folk* (New York: The Modern Library, 2003).
Eze, Emmanuel Chukwudi, ed. *Race and the Enlightenment: A Reader* (Oxford: Wiley-Blackwell, 1997).
Foucault, Michel. *Abnormal: Lectures at the Collège de France 1974–1975*, translated by Graham Burchell (New York: Picador, 1999).
———. *Society Must Be Defended: Lectures at the College de France 1975–1976* (New York: Picador, 1997).

Gawrylewski, Andrea. "The Case for Antiracism." *Scientific American*, Summer 2021.

Girvan, E., and H. J. Marek. "Psychological and Structural Bias in Civil Jury Awards." *Journal of Aggression, Conflict and Peace Research* 8, no. 4 (2016): 247–257.

Goffman, Erving. *Stigma: Notes on the Management of Spoiled Identity* (New York: Simon & Schuster, 1986).

Goldstein, Joel K. "Not Hearing History: A Critique of Chief Justice Roberts's Reinterpretation of Brown." *Ohio State Law Journal* 69 (2008): 791.

Harman, Graham. *Tool Being: Heidegger and the Metaphysics of Objects* (Chicago: Open Court, 2002).

Haslanger, Sally. "Gender and Race: (What) Are They? (What) Do We Want Them to Be?" *Noûs* 34, no. 1 (2000): 31–55.

———. "Tracing the Sociopolitical Reality of Race." In *What is Race* (Cambridge: Oxford University Press, 2019).

Heidegger, Martin. *Basic Writings: From Being and Time (1927) to the Task of Thinking (1964)*, edited by David Farrell Krell (New York: Harper Collins Publishers Inc., 1993).

———. *Being and Time*, translated by Joan Stambaugh (Albany: SUNY Press, 2010).

———. *Being and Time*, translated by John MacQuarrie and Edward Robinson (New York: Harper Perennial, 1962).

———. *History of the Concept of Time: Prolegomena*, translated by Theodore Kisiel (Bloomington: Indiana University Press, 1985).

———. *Ontology: The Hermeneutics of Facticity*, translated by John van Buren (Blomington: Indiana University Press, 1999).

———. *The Basic Problems of Phenomenology*, translated by Albert Hofstadter (Bloomington: Indiana University Press, 1982).

Hull, Gordon. "Equitable Relief as a Relay Between Juridical and Biopower: The Case of School Desegregation" *Continental Philosophy Review* 50 (2017): 225.

Isenberg, Nancy. *White Trash: The 400-Year Untold History of Class in America* (New York: Viking, 2016).

Johnson, Jacqueline. "Mass Incarceration: a Contemporary Mechanism of Racialization in the United States." *Gonzaga Law Review* 47 (2012): 301–318.

Jones, Jacqueline. *A Dreadful Deceit: The Myth of Race From the Colonial Era to Obama's America* (New York: Basic Books, 2013).

Kaufmann, Walter, ed. *The Portable Nietzsche* (New York: Penguin Books, 1982).

Kendi, Ibram X. *Stamped From the Beginning: The Definitive History of Racist Ideas in America* (New York: Nation Books, 2016).

Keyes, Allison. "A Long-Lost Manuscript Contains a Searing Eyewitness Account of the Tulsa Race Massacre of 1921." *smithsonianmag.com*, May 27, 2016.

Kleinman, Arthur, and Rachel Hall-Clifford. "Stigma: A Social, Cultural and Moral Process." *Journal of Epidemiology & Community Health* 63, no. 6 (2009): 418–419.

López, Ian Haney. "Race and Colorblindness After Hernandez and Brown." *Chicana/o Latina/o Law Review* 25, no. 1 (2005): 61.

MacKinnon, Catherine A. *Toward a Feminist Theory of the State* (Cambridge: Harvard University Press, 1989).
Manne, Kate. *Down Girl: The Logic of Misogyny* (Oxford: Oxford University Press, 2018).
———. "Humanism." *Social Theory and Practice* 42, no. 2 (2016): 389–415.
———. "In Ferguson and Beyond, Punishing Humanity." *New York Times*, October 12, 2014.
McWhorter, Ladelle. "Racism and Biopower." In *On Race and Racism in America: Confessions in Philosophy*, edited by Roy Martinez (University Park: Pennsylvania State University Press, 2010).
———. *Racism and Sexual Oppression in Anglo-America: A Genealogy* (Indianapolis: Indiana University Press, 2009).
Mills, Charles. *Black Rights/White Wrongs: The Critique of Racial Liberalism* (New York: Oxford University Press, 2017).
———. *The Racial Contract* (Ithaca, NY: Cornell University Press, 1997).
Mitchell, Sarah. "Theorizing Mass Incarceration: Augmenting Foucault." *OSWEGO* (2014).
Morrison, Steven R. "Will to Power, Will to Reality, and Racial Profiling: How the White Male Dominant Power Structure Creates Itself as Law Abiding Citizen Through the Creation of Black as Criminal." *Northwestern Journal of Law & Society Pol* 2 (2007): 63.
Morrison, Toni. *The Bluest Eye* (New York: Vintage Books, 1970).
———. "The Site of Memory." In *Inventing the Truth: The Art and Craft of Memoir*, edited by William Zinsser, 2nd ed. (Boston; New York: Houghton Mifflin, 1995).
Natapoff, Alexandra. *Punishment Without Crime: How Our Massive Misdemeanor System Traps the Innocent and Makes America More Unequal* (New York: Basic Books, 2018), 174.
Pateman, Carol. *The Sexual Contract* (Stanford, CA: Stanford University Press, 1988).
Pateman, Carol, and Charles Mills. *Contract & Domination* (Cambridge: Polity, 2007).
Peller, Gary. *Critical Race Consciousness* (Boulder: Paradigm Publishers, 2012).
———. "Privilege 104." *GEO. L. J.* 883-920 (2016).
Polizzi, David. *A Phenomenological Hermeneutic of Antiblack Racism in the Autobiography of Malcolm X* (Lanham, MD: Lexington Books, 2019).
Powell, John. "Parents Involved: The Mantle of Brown, the Shadow of Plessy." *University Louisville Law Review* 46 (2008): 631.
Rodriguez, Richard. *Days of Obligation: An Argument With My Mexican Father* (New York: Penguin, 1992).
Rothstein, Richard. *The Color of Law* (New York: Liveright Publishing, 2017).
Sheth, Falguni A. *Toward a Political Philosophy of Race* (New York: SUNY Press, 2009).
Smith, David. "Paradoxes of Dehumanization." *Social Theory and Practice*, January 2016.

Smith, David Livingstone. *Less Than Human: Why We Demean, Enslave, and Exterminate Others* (New York: St. Martin's Press, 2011).
Taylor, James. *Techno-Racism: Heidegger's Philosophy of Technology and Critical Philosophies of Race* (Doctoral Dissertation, Duquesne University, 2016).
Turner, Ronald. "Plessy 2.0." *Lewis & Clark Law Review* 13 (Winter 2009): 861–919.
Warren, Calvin. *Ontological Terror: Blackness, Nihilism, and Emancipation* (Durham, NC: Duke University Press, 2018).
West, Cornel. *Prophesy Deliverance: An Afro-American Revolutionary Christianity* (Louisville: Westminster John Knox Press, 1982).
Wildman, Stephanie M. "The Persistence of White Privilege." *Washington University Journal Law & Pol'y* 18 (2005): 245.
Williams, Patricia J. *The Alchemy of Race and Rights: Diary of a Law Professor* (Cambridge: Harvard University Press, 1991).
Wriggins, Jennifer. "Tort, Race, and the Value of Injury: 1900–1949." *Howard Law Journal* 49 (2005): 99.
Yancy, George. *Black Bodies, White Gazes: The Continuing Significance of Race in America*, 2nd ed. (New York: Rowman & Littlefield, 2017).
Yoshino, Kenji. *Covering: The Hidden Assault on Our Civil Rights* (New York: Random House, 2006).
Zack, Naomi. *White Privilege and Black Rights: The Injustice of U.S. Police Racial Profiling and Homicide* (Lanham, MD: Rowman & Littlefield, 2015).

Index

Adarand v. Peña, 54–56, 111
affirmative action, 54, 57, 61, 117, 122
Americans with Disabilities Act, 119–21

being. *See* Heideggerian ontology
being-in-the-world. *See* Heideggerian ontology
Black being-in-the-world. *See* blackness
Black Lives Matter, 88
blackness: black being-in-the-world, 89–98; black world, 56, 97–98; brand of, 23–25, 27–29, 33–34, 43–51, 63–67, 87–89, 113, 127
brands, 21–22; gender as brand, 25–26; ontological brands, 21–23, 27–29; race as brand, 23–25, 33–47, 49–51, 58, 84–89, 121; socioeconomic class as brand, 26–29; unbrandedness, 2, 4, 22–29, 35–38, 42, 44–45, 48, 58, 64–65, 83–102, 115–16, 123, 129

Civil Rights Era, 3, 50, 52–53
class, socioeconomic, 45–48; brand of. *See* brands, socioeconomic class as brand
colonialism, 24, 34, 38–40
colorblindness, 51–52, 54–55, 61–62, 67, 112, 114, 128

Constitution, United States, 4, 47, 55–57, 61–62, 101, 112–13, 121; Equal Protection Clause, 54–55, 58, 59, 61, 121
disability, 35, 119–21
discrimination, 3–4, 55–56, 58–63, 112–13, 115, 119–22
diversity, 54, 58–62, 122
Dred Scott v. Sandford, 47, 49
dualism, 91–92

Enlightenment, 4, 8, 33, 38–40, 43, 100
equality, 4, 8, 35, 37–40, 47–49, 51–53, 55, 57–58, 60, 62–63, 65, 84, 93, 100, 111–12, 114, 129; ontological equality, 118–22, 129
Equal Protection Clause. *See* Constitution, United States

familiarity. *See* Heideggerian ontology
feminist philosophy, 41, 96, 115, 122

gender, 25–26, 36, 86, 92, 94, 118
genealogy, 4, 33–35, 37

Heidegger, Martin, 7–8
Heideggerian ontology: being in the world, 9–10, 22–25, 57, 83;

familiarity, 12–16, 36–37, 42, 66, 83, 85–86, 94; mere things, 8–12, 25, 51, 59, 83; modes of being, 8; persons, 9–10; tools, 10–16, 23–25, 33–34, 37, 43–45, 50–51, 83, 85–86, 89, 94–95, 101, 113; unfamiliarity, 13, 14, 21, 67, 94–95; worlds, 10–16, 21–23, 34–37, 49–51, 66–67, 83–85, 87–91, 97–98

implicit bias, 87, 98
injustice. *See* justice
intersectionality, 27–29

Jim Crow, 3, 49–50, 52–53, 56, 60, 63, 65, 128
justice, 2, 52–53; injustice, 53; ontological justice, 4, 5, 111, 113–15, 118–19, 122, 129; racial injustice, 43, 53, 56, 87, 113–18; racial justice, 3–5, 52–57, 62, 84, 113–15, 118–19, 122, 129

law, 2–5, 11, 33, 45–63, 65–67, 83, 111–23, 127–29
liberalism, 24, 30, 40–41, 43, 58, 84, 115, 119
lynching, 49–50, 63

masculinity, 26, 30
meritocracy, 27, 40, 58, 111
multiculturalism, 117

nonwhiteness. *See* whiteness
normality, 3, 28, 36–37, 41–42, 50, 83, 85, 87, 95–96, 99, 101

ontological branding. *See* brands
ontological equality. *See* equality
ontological justice. *See* justice
ontological power, 4, 23, 26, 36, 47, 88, 90, 119, 123
ontological privilege, 5, 23–24, 27–29, 48, 67, 85, 92, 98–99, 102, 115, 117, 129; privilege as right to harm, 5, 45–47, 49, 64, 66–67, 116, 127–28
ontological subordination, 24, 26, 38, 44, 65, 84–85, 87, 89–98, 101, 113, 118, 122
ontology. *See* Heideggerian ontology

Parents Involved in Community Schools v. Seattle School District No. 1, 54, 58, 60–61, 100
patriarchy, 25–26, 34, 96
personhood, 2, 4–5, 7–9, 23–27, 33, 37–38, 40–42, 48–49, 57, 84, 87–89, 92, 94, 118, 127; person simpliciter, 2, 4, 7, 8, 22–29, 33–37, 41, 44–45, 48, 51, 64, 66, 83–88, 118, 127
phenomenology, 5, 7, 35, 44, 89, 92, 93
Plessy v. Ferguson, 49, 51, 60–61
police brutality, 62–63, 65, 98, 128
postracialism, 57, 67
privilege. *See* ontological privilege
punishment, 5, 21–22, 25–26, 45, 47, 50, 63, 65, 90, 127–29

queerness, 23, 26, 35

race: race as mere fact, 48, 52, 58, 83; race as tool, 21, 24–25, 36–37, 40, 86, 101
racial injustice. *See* justice
racial justice. *See* justice
racism, 5n1, 42, 53, 60, 88, 115, 118–19; antiblack racism, 25, 33–34, 98; scientific racism, 38, 42, 50
Reconstruction, 3, 49, 52–53
Redemption, 49
Regents of the University of California v. Bakke, 119
reparations, 115
right to harm. *See* ontological privilege

Schuette v. Coalition to Defend Affirmative Action, 54, 61–62, 119
scientific racism. *See* racism

segregation, 59–62, 112
self-defense, 45–46, 65, 100–101, 128
slavery, 4, 33, 38, 40–49, 53, 56, 64, 93, 96, 112, 128

technology, 3, 7, 39
Tennessee v. Lane, 121
tools. *See* Heideggerian ontology

unbrandedness. *See* brands
unfamiliarity. *See* Heideggerian ontology

(white) America, 1–2, 5, 24–25, 33–37, 43–67, 84, 87–89, 93, 95, 98–101, 112–22, 127–29

whiteness, 2–3, 5, 7–8, 24–25, 27–28, 33–38, 40–42, 44–45, 47–48, 51–52, 58, 60, 65–67, 83, 85, 87, 89, 98–101, 111–17, 119, 121–23, 127; nonwhiteness, 3, 24–25, 33–34, 36–38, 40, 47–48, 58, 66, 83, 114, 119, 121–22, 127
white supremacy, 2–5, 7–8, 33–34, 37–43, 49–52, 58, 63, 66–67, 87, 90, 95–97, 99, 111–14, 116, 118–19, 121–22, 128–29
womanhood, 25, 27–28, 34, 64, 65, 86, 96
world. *See* Heideggerian ontology

About the Author

Bonard Iván Molina García is an international arbitration attorney (FCIArb) and independent scholar based in Washington D.C.

www.ingramcontent.com/pod-product-compliance
Lightning Source LLC
Chambersburg PA
CBHW020126010526
44115CB00008B/992